V O I C E S *o f*
S TEVENAGE

Roy Gates in the woodyard at Trinity Road, with a traction engine, *c.* 1930.

VOICES *of* STEVENAGE

MARGARET ASHBY

The History Press

First published in 1999 by Tempus Publishing

Reprinted in 2013 by
The History Press
The Mill, Brimscombe Port,
Stroud, Gloucestershire, GL5 2QG
www.thehistorypress.co.uk

British Library Cataloguing in Publication Data.
A catalogue record for this book is available from the British Library.

ISBN 978 0 7524 1593 2

Typesetting and origination by
Tempus Publishing Limited
Printed and bound in Great Britain by
Marston Book Services Limited, Didcot

Other books by Margaret Ashby:

The Book of Stevenage
The Book of the River Lea
Forster Country
Stevenage: history and guide
Stevenage Past
A Hertfordshire Christmas

Stevenage coat of arms and motto.

CONTENTS

INTRODUCTION

Oral history, based on the spoken memories of older people in a community, gives an opportunity for everyone to contribute. Some of my previous books have received the comment, 'This is not the real history, it is not about ordinary people.' Leaving aside the argument as to whether anyone is 'ordinary', this book is different from the others, as it recounts the experiences of Stevenage people during the past century, in their own words.

This book has come about following two Cambridge University Board of Continuing Education courses which I tutored in 1997-8 and 1998-9. They were aimed specifically at collecting the memories of older people of old Stevenage, before their culture is totally assimilated into that of the new. The venue, at Holy Trinity church, in the High Street, was convenient for a number of people who lived within walking distance, but we also drew in others from further afield, including some new town residents.

The resulting collection of tapes is a fascinating and invaluable record but, it must be stressed, it is not in any way a scientifically calculated sample, nor a representative cross-section of today's population. But it does reflect, in microcosm, the different cultures of old and new. Those from old Stevenage, who had shared childhood and schooldays over seventy or eighty years ago, in a small country town on the Great North Road could see, in their collective mind's eye, images of long vanished rectors, school teachers, fields, lanes, and farms. Those from new Stevenage, from disparate backgrounds, who had been plunged into an alien environment without the familiar landmarks and traditions of a previous existence, had created their own history. The two are merging now but separate traditions still exist.

Anyone writing a history of Stevenage is confronted with the problem of the break in continuity which occurred following the 1946 act which designated Stevenage Britain's first New Town. The enormity and speed of the change from a small country town of 6,000 in 1946 to a borough of nearly 80,000 fifty years later, is something that all of us here are still living through. In terms of writing a balanced history of the town, this represents a conflict impossible to resolve satisfactorily.

The weight of history lies with the old town, which has been chronicled since Saxon times: the majority of the present population is now a result of the new town. More has changed, more rapidly, in the last fifty years than in the previous one thousand. Since the main purpose of oral history is to record the memories of an older generation, this book reflects the life of this century, the years of a continuing rural tradition, the distortions of the two world wars, the break with the past as the new town was built and its continuing expansion, with the concomitant disappearance of the landscape of history. Yet, as the voices of 'ordinary' people relate their experiences, their hopes, fears, joys and sorrows, it becomes clear how much they have in common.

Converting the spoken word to the written presents its own problems. To make these spoken memories easy on the eye, as opposed to the ear, I have had to add punctuation and to leave out characteristic features such as, 'um', 'er', 'you know', 'and that', 'you see', and so on. Nor can the written word capture the all-important intonation, which adds so much meaning. The words lie cold on the page, tidied up and devoid of hesitation or emphasis, missing the warmth and humour, the knowing looks, and the unspoken understandings. The written word cannot reproduce local accents. The Stevenage version of the Hertfordshire dialect, never perhaps very distinct, has long been under siege from London, only thirty miles away along the Great North Road.

Even so, newcomers to Stevenage have been confused by the local speech-patterns, the use of the word 'old' being the best-known example. 'When someone told me about a "little old boy", said one newcomer, 'I expected to see a short, elderly gentleman, so I was quite surprised to find a baby in a pushchair.' There are many variations in the use of 'old' and to understand them it is often necessary to know the context or hear the intonation. It can be used to express affection, as, 'I know old George would help.' Equally, it can indicate dislike, 'That old cat has dug up my flower bed.' Often it is used merely for emphasis but the variations are subtle and not easily grasped by those not brought up among them.

Another common usage is 'that' to replace 'it', 'he', or, 'she', as in, 'I had a fox terrier once. That could catch any rat,' or 'He left the car by the gate and when he came back that had run down the road.' A local expression which I particularly like, is, 'You may depend,' spoken in a peculiarly comfortable voice which makes the listener feel that all is right with the world, for example: 'If he was ever late home from school, you may depend I was too.' Often it is used in answer to a question, 'Did you have maypole dancing at your school?' 'I can't really remember, but you may depend we did.' 'You may depend' does not transfer effectively to the printed page; it needs to be heard. Another rural expression, now fast disappearing, but still occasionally used is 'at that time of day' meaning 'then' or 'in those days.'

As for local accents and differentiating between north Hertfordshire and the various London voices, suffice it to say that, whereas people from away cannot tell them apart, to those living here they are as different as chalk and cheese, and one grates harshly on the ear of the other.

Whilst acknowledging all the inherent limitations of transferring the spoken word to the printed page, this book is an attempt to put on permanent accessible record a little of the life of Stevenage in the twentieth century, as told by 'ordinary' people. Through the medium of print, although the voices will be stilled, their words will live on.

Albert Street celebrates the end of the war.

ACKNOWLEDGEMENTS

More than most, this book is the result of teamwork and the contributions of a great many people. First and foremost, I extend very grateful thanks to all those who agreed to be interviewed and recorded and whose names appear, with their memories, throughout the book. Many also lent photographs, which help bring the printed page to life. Patricia and Ian Aspinall, Peg Charlton, Gerald Graves, Bob, Len and Roy North and John Richardson also kindly helped with photographs and information. Sadly, two of those who made recordings have since died: Thelma Bartholomew and Arthur Cotts. I should like to express my sympathy to their families and to thank them for allowing me to include extracts from their recordings in this book.

Secondly, I should like to thank the students of my Friday morning Oral History class, who worked so hard on the other side of the microphone, interviewing, recording, and transcribing and sometimes contributing their own memories: John Amess, Joan Amis, Jean Baker, Kate Cope, Chris Cox, Sheila Davies, Roy Findley, Dorothy Gorbing, Sybil Graham, Joan Hale, Phil Ibbotson, Eileen Martin, Reg Milliner, and Wilf Neilson.

Thirdly, I acknowledge with gratitude the work of Joan Amis, who transcribed many of the tapes, Roy Findley, who undertook most of the liaison with contributors, Stella Kestin who typed the manuscript, Betty Game, who assisted with editing and Steve Hodges, who once again rescued me from the machinations of modern technology.

CHAPTER 1

Childhood and Youth

M.A. Gates with his cousin, Maud Day, in a donkey cart, 1896.

Penny Ice

On a Sunday afternoon, we used to go down and sit on the Six Hills and the ice-cream man used to come and he'd sell out, because all us kids used to say, 'Got a penny?' so we could go and buy an ice cream. And we used to take the numbers of the cars and see who would get the most numbers at the end of the day.

Elsie Hills

The Ovaltinies

We had a radio and we used to listen to the Ovaltinies, Happy Girls and Boys, you know. That was Sunday nights. There was no television then, but we used to enjoy it. There wasn't much going on, not as a child, I don't think, really. Oh, a top and little games and a lot of skipping and hopscotch and that sort of thing out in the Back Lane and 'mothers and fathers' down the Shepherds yard.

Kathleen Jackson

Unlucky Break

We couldn't paddle in the pond, it was really too deep unfortunately. If we had a terrific storm that pond used to fill up and it would overflow and the road out here used to get flooded right over into Holy Trinity church and it used to be quite slippy as well. It was on this church wall that I fell off and broke my arm, on the Coach and Horses side. I was actually sitting there and some of the boys that were playing around came and touched me and I fell backwards and broke my arm on a tree stump.

E. Woods

The Murky Pond

The only pond I ever swam in was the brickyard pond at Fishers Green. There were two big ponds there. We used to swim in the back one that was pretty deep and it had a sort of circular clearing in the rushes and that had some huge pike in there, over three foot long. I remember one boy got bitten on the thigh, it took a bit out of him. That's the only swimming I ever did, in that old pond. It was a bit murky.

Roy Gates

I Couldn't Wait to Get Away

My mother's family went back in Stevenage to about 1500, both on my mother's father's and my mother's mother's side. They were really generations ensconced in Stevenage. My father's family came from Newmarket. There wasn't much to do but I very much enjoyed as a boy, with my friends, just going across the fields birds' nesting and going down to Fairlands Farm and going to the pond and trying to catch a few sticklebacks. I couldn't wait to get away from the house in Haycroft Road to be perfectly honest, that was prison as far as I was concerned. Because the front room was a shop I couldn't really have any friends in, there wasn't anywhere to have friends, there was just a kitchen and a scullery behind the shop and two bedrooms upstairs. It was gaslight, we didn't have any electricity. There was nowhere one could bring one's friends, so one got out.

Don Hills

Pleasure and Pain

I was born on Fishers Green in the centre one of three cottages. It was a nice house and my mother started off her married life there, but the drains were so bad that she was afraid because when she was a girl she lost her twin brother with diphtheria. So she was very frightened and, very foolishly really, she moved down to this little cottage in Coreys Mill, which hadn't got any facilities at all, no outside loo, no sink. But Fishers Green was lovely in those days. It was just a wild green with two ponds, and Mr Moules's farm and you could go across there with your jug and get some fresh milk in the morning. Bullrushes and fish were in the ponds and there were lovely harebells. It was very pretty really. And it was right next to the railway. When we were children at Coreys Mill we used to spend many days by the railway watching the trains go by. We were told not to go over the bridge to Fishers Green to play with the children there because there was this brickall, a pond that they used when they made the bricks over Fishers Green and it used to get very thick with weeds. I know one or two boys lost their lives by getting in, so we were warned not to go, and the boys were warned not to walk across the railway bridge, but they did. And we were warned not to cross the railway line but we did. We were disobedient many a time. Further down by the wood, getting on to Wymondley, there was a pit where they dug out material for the railway line and we played down there. And there were beautiful blue butterflies. We used to go into the woods quite freely and sometimes you'd see an old tramp, from the road, and he would be having his fire and cooking his meal. But they never said anything to us. We were never afraid.

Lily Glazebrook

Friendly Gangs

The Trinity Road gang used to come to Fishers Green. We used to go up and play cricket against them, and football. There was the Trinity Road gang, the Haycroft Road gang, the Walkern Road gang and then there was the Fishers Green Road gang.

E. Woods

It Was All Countryside

I was born in Green Street and then, of course, there were all fields round us. We used to go through the alley to Madgin's field, which is all built on now. We never used to play a lot in the road because we always had the fields all round us. We always had somewhere to play and when we used to go up over the bridge into Fairview Road there'd be all fields up there – it was all countryside. We were free to go on our

Gates's field and the steps leading to Chequers Bridge Road.

own, because there were six of us in the family and then you had friends – we used to have some good times.

Mrs I. Cotts

The Biggest Thing in My Life

The scouts had several meeting places. The first one I can remember was in Sish Lane, in the drill hall there, which is now the Knitting Company. It used to be a drill hall for soldiers in the First World War. The scout meeting was the biggest thing in my life, waiting for the next week to come round, because I enjoyed it so much.

Norman Palmer

Traction Engines

I remember when they used to have two steam engines in the woodyard. Before that they had four or six horses to bring the logs and trees, in and then they graduated to steam engines, traction engines. I've got a picture of me by one of them when I was about five, I think. The works were run by a huge stationary steam engine and it had a fly wheel. I think the fly wheel was fifteen foot across. My uncle, Wally Racher used to run it. I used to go up there and he showed me how it worked. And they had that huge crane that used to pull the logs up off the timber wagons and swing round and put them by the saws to cut it up.

Roy Gates

Expensive Woodcut

On the other side of Trinity Road was the woodyard. As they cut all the trees they used to bring the sawdust out into one of the fields which belonged to Mr Gates and there were great heaps of sawdust. Of course, us kids hardly ever went to the seaside, we thought that was sand, so we used to go in and play in it. We'd got our Wellingtons on one day and we were playing all in it and of course the sawdust got all down into our Wellingtons and we couldn't get them off. When we got home our mothers had to cut the Wellingtons to get them off.

Elsie Hills

A Nightingale Sang

Later, the scouts met in a loft in Mr Scoot's yard in Julian's Road. From there, we went up to a place opposite the Marquess of Granby, where there were some buildings belonging to the Barclay family, which they let us use. Then we met in a hut that was built for us, in a field belonging to Mr Barclay. We used to camp up there at weekends, in Whitney Wood and we used to hear the nightingales. Wonderful!

Norman Palmer

Playing Games

You could play out in the dark nights, because nobody was worried about you then, and we used to play hide and seek, nothing outstanding, just ordinary children's games. We had a lot of camps in the logs in the woodyard, especially if we didn't want anybody to find us and we knew where to go. If we'd got to do any shopping or anything, we used to say, 'Come on, let's go up the field.' And we all used to go. It's surprising those logs never fell on us, really.

Elsie Hills

Brothers in the First Stevenage Scouts. From the left: Len North (cub), Roy North (Rover), Bob North (scout), 1938.

We Respected the Police

The police were quite good. They used to come round on their bikes, especially bonfire night, to make sure you weren't letting fireworks off beforehand, there was none of that, nor after fireworks night. They were fair but as I grew up, so things gradually got to a certain stage, I suppose it was the beginning of this era, where there was more trouble, and you got different people coming into the town, they then used to be a little more strict with us. But as teenage boys, still at school, we got on with the police all right. They never used to worry us at all. When I was a boy we used to go roller skating up the High Street of a night-time when the lorries had finished going through and no one was out on the road. The only thing that came out was

Mr Allison's pony and trap, he used to come down the road. But we used to go skating up and down the High Street, go into Davis and Mindenhall's garage and get the skates oiled up and then go off again.

E. Woods

Energetic Games

We played marbles and spinning tops and we ran up and down the road with wooden hoops. I was very lucky, I had an iron one with a little sort of scoop thing that you held against it, to keep it going so that you didn't have to keep it going with your hand. When we got a little bit older, we moved down the greens on Letchmore Road where we played our cricket and

Roy Findley in his garden in Albert Street, *c.* 1930.

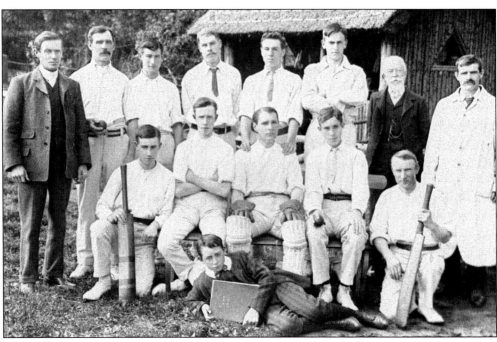

Graveley cricket team. Standing, second from right is Charles Poyntz-Stewart of Chesfield Park. His son, Neil is standing fourth from left.

14

generally ran around and had fist fights and then when we got a bit older still, we went to what is now Pound Avenue. There was a field there, where we played cricket and football.

Don Hills

Lewin Waby's Toy Shop

I had a particular interest in toy soldiers and received a fort as a present, on which I displayed the riflemen and guards and set my cannons outside, firing matchsticks at them, with the cavalry advancing towards the drawbridge. Most of the toys were bought from Lewin Waby's shop in the High Street, where his quite tiny area was a mass of toys and games stacked to the ceiling. The opposite half of his shop sold hardware and crockery. Next door, Sharp's specialised in the sale of Dinky Toys, Meccano, and train sets, and further down the street, Boorman's sold bicycles, bells and torches in one window and a range of toys, prams and push chairs in the other.

Roy Findley

Halfpenny Sweets

We used to run from Huntingdon Road, Fishers Green to St Nicholas' school, at the bottom of the Avenue. And then we used to play hide and seek on the way to school, in the old Council Yard in Julian's Road, where Lincoln's Tyre Yard is now. They used to keep all the horses and carts there. We'd be late for school, go and spend our

Stevenage Brownies. Back row, left to right: -?-, -?-, Daphne Wellard, -?-, -?-. Middle row: -?-, Joan Rosendale, -?-, Phyllis Chance. Seated on chairs: -?-, Vera Males, -?-, Mrs Dorothy Griffith, Miss Miriam French, Freda Hawkins, June Berry, Una Wittering. Seated on ground: -?-, Margaret Hawkins, -?-, Betty Johnson.

15

Stevenage's famous Six Hills beside the Great North Road, c. 1910.

halfpenny in Millie Kefford's sweet shop or Scarborough's shop on the corner of Nottingham Road.

Roy Gates

Camping at Chesfield

Mrs Poyntz-Stewart allowed us to go camping at Chesfield Park. We usually walked there, with a trek cart. We used to play cricket there and also, I can remember playing cricket against the Graveley side.

Norman Palmer

Timber wagons

The timber came from all the woods about, mostly the estates, like Weston Park and Hitch Wood, all around, just as far as you could pull them with the horses and carts. That was how it all started, with timber wagons. We used to go to Hitch Wood

to get beansticks for Letchmore Road school, and we used to get beech nuts up there, used to be some lovely beech trees on the right hand side there, up the hill.

Roy Gates

Magic Lanterns

Another little thing that I belonged to, held at the old Parish Hall, was the Young Crusaders. Lantern slides, magic lantern slides, a treat, absolutely fascinating. Any youngster could go. They didn't turn anyone away, you didn't have to be a churchgoer.

Don Hills

Belonging

I was a Brownie and I belonged to the Band of Hope. I think it was every Thursday evening we used to go, and we had all games, at the Bunyan Chapel,

16

bottom of Basil's Road, in the hall there. Then on Mondays we used to go to the Wesleyan Chapel and they had the same sort of thing.

Mrs I. Cotts

A Trip to the Coal Mines

We went on various camping trips, usually by coach. Once we went to Doncaster, where we went down the coal mines, then went on to Whitby, had a camping holiday there and moved on to the Lake District where the rain absolutely washed us out so we had to go and sleep in a barn. We also climbed Langdale Pikes, then went on Buxton in Derbyshire, a lovely area. We did one trip with the Rovers travelling overnight, driving by moonlight, quite a new experience, seeing the dawn. We also used to camp

at Stagenhoe Park and at Walkern and down the lane that used to lead from Sish Lane into Shephall. There was a site there, near Shephall.

Norman Palmer

Nasty Tricks

We used to play parcels, fill a parcel up full of horse dung and some old girl would take it home. We used to tie knockers together too, two side-by-side doors. You're supposed to leave the string slack, knock at a door and of course, when they opened their door it knocked the other one and so it went on. We did that once to one house up there – we tied it too tight and of course, when the the door was opened, it pulled the knocker off!

Roy Gates

Alleyne's Grammar School scouts, *c.* 1919. Cyril Richardson is third from the right, back row.

17

Advertisement for Shelford Record baker, 1930s.

Our Favourite Policeman

We had one policeman who was our favourite, a Mr Haggar. He had a scar on the side of his face, a red scar from birth and he was a policeman and a half. He kept us children in good control and if he saw you doing anything, he would come up and tell you. But if you did anything really bad in his eyes, that you knew you shouldn't be doing, you never got a talking to, you got his gloves around your head. He'd slap your ear with his gloves and you daren't go home and tell your Dad because he'd give you another one for getting into trouble.

E. Woods

Gang Show

In my scouting days we used to collect eggs from people in private houses, to take over to the Hitchin Hospital. We'd go on the double-decker bus. And of course, we gave various shows, gang shows and otherwise. We did some at the Town Hall and also at Walkern, at the village hall. Once, I had to sing a song, something like, 'I'm a Little Prairie Flower.'

Norman Palmer

Early Rising

The dairy was in Albert Street and then there was the stable for two horses. Dad kept his cart in the double gates in the Back Lane, as we call it, Church Lane is the posh name. The horses would wake him up in the morning, about half past four, for feeding – you didn't need an alarm clock with them – and then we started. I'd probably go out about half past six in the morning, with the afternoon before's milk. I'd bike over Fairview Road and then Pound Avenue and back and then go and meet him at the bottom of Pin Green and then I'd do a few roads helping before I left for school.

Kathleen Jackson

We Were Never Bored

Years ago there weren't all these facilities, we had to make our own pleasures. They talk about being bored now and getting up to crime, but we used to make our own enjoyment. One of the fields that we used to use was all holes where they'd dug the clay out for the brickyards, and there was another on the other side of the railway line. There used to be a big dell over there and they used to call that field 'Shelford's Dell.' Shelfords had a big bakehouse opposite

Trinity church, next to the Motor Company. They kept, oh, I don't know, a dozen horses and carts for the bread rounds. They used to go round a lot of the villages.

Roy Gates

Shepherd's Yard

My aunt lived in Belmont Cottages in Church Lane, opposite Fishy Furr's at the back and we used to go down there a lot and play. We used to play down at Shepherd's Yard and have a bonfire down there on Guy Fawkes night. We had an old desk to play with under the plum tree in the garden; where it came from I don't know, it was a proper desk. We used to play out there and we used to have some lovely plums. Everybody used to look forward to having some of them.

Kathleen Jackson

Snow Drifts

I can remember a time when Walkern Road and all the other roads were covered up with drifts of snow, right up above the hedges and we walked along the top of it. I had so much hot-ache in my feet I had to come home to be thawed out.

Norman Palmer

Queen's Scout

I was in the Third Stevenage, Holy Trinity, Scout Troop, when Bill

Hopkinson founded it in 1946/47. He was a curate here. The Third Stevenage was really formed from Trinity church choir. At that time the rector was John Humphrey King. He did a lot for scouting and made quite an impression on a lot of us. There was a very strange quirk of fate when I was wanting to become a King's Scout. In February 1952 I was doing the last badge, which was the Ambulance Badge, which is very important and I passed it one day and the king died the next. And so I didn't become a King's Scout, I became a Queen's Scout, but I happened to be the first one ever. But it did get me an invitation to the coronation, to work with Gaumont British News, working with the scouts up at Westminster Abbey and at the Home

Joan (left) and Kathleen Phipps in their Aunt Mollie's garden at Belmont Cottages, Back Lane, 1930s.

The Christmas crib at Holy Trinity church, made and carved by Bert Weaver, 1956.

Roy Findley, aged nine, walking along the High Street near Lewin Waby's toy shop.

Office across the road, so I had some wonderful experiences then.

John Austin

Christmas Memories

The Children's Corner at Holy Trinity was close to the porch entrance and was where the Biblical stories were read to us and we received instruction and collected religious picture stamps for attendance, to go in to an album. At Christmas, naturally, a nativity was displayed there. At home the front room became decorated with holly, balanced on the picture frames, and paper chains were draped across the ceiling, having been made from the packets of coloured lengths of paper, folded and glued, usually with flour paste and linked together. There was a small tree, with the fragile, coloured glass decorations hanging on it and cotton wool pieces creating the effect of snow. There were no electric lights because we still had gas lamps. Christmas dinner was turkey or a plump chicken, and this – different from today – was a special treat from the roast beef we normally had on Sundays.

Roy Findley

Kind Deeds at Christmas

At Christmas time the scouts collected money among themselves and we bought coal, logs and chocolates which we took to the old people in Back Lane, especially the almshouses, but we also used to get a list from the Council of anybody else that needed it.

Norman Palmer

CHAPTER 2

Home and Family

Trinity Road. Mrs Roy Gates, with Jane and Alan on bicycles and Ann with Shetland pony, *c.* 1959.

Cakes and Ale

A lot of the houses in Trinity Road belonged to a Mr Blow, who was related to the Blow's cake shop people. He used to charge my mum 5/- a week. There wasn't much in the house, it was a very cold house, but we were happy in it. We had lovely fun in it, at Christmas time. A lot of the men used to go down to the Chequers public house, that was their local, and my mum used to put a lovely spread on and my father used to bring maybe six couples back. One Christmas, Mr Tooley, who used to live in Trinity Road and Mr Ireton, who used to play the piano-accordian, they came back that night and we were in what we called the front room then. You were only in there high days and holidays, you couldn't go in there any other time. Under that front room there was the cellar – terrific big cellar it was and this Mr Tooley, he was such a big man and he was dancing away there and all of a sudden he went through the floor boards. But it just finished up happy, you know, nobody was worried, he didn't hurt himself or anything. Our house was a public house before – there were loads of public houses up there.

Elsie Hills

Clean Inside and Out

I was born on 9 February, 1920 at 49, Letchmore Road, in Coronation Cottages, opposite the Dun Cow. The

Janet and Peter Charlton outside their grandparents' home at Coronation Cottages, 43, Letchmore Road.

Mr Joseph Johnson, Louise and Joey at Bell Plash, *c.* 1925.

cottages reached from where the White Horse is now to the top of Grove Road. They had lovely, long gardens at the back. There was a whole string of cottages, the small ones were at the top and the bigger ones were at the bottom. We were at the bottom. We had three bedrooms and three downstairs rooms and an outside toilet. We didn't have a bathroom, but we managed with a tin bath. We had to be very conservative with water. Mum had a copper in the scullery and we used to fill the copper to heat the water for a bath. We didn't have a bath every day like you do now, or a shower every day, but we had a bath every week – and a dose of Syrup of Figs.

Louise Richards

Bath Night by the Fire

Outside hung the zinc bath which was brought in each Friday and placed in the scullery in summer and in front of the living room fire in winter (it burned you on one side and froze you on the other). The copper had to be lit to heat the water, and you didn't have a fresh lot each. Being the child I was lucky and came first. When I was older and had to fill and empty the bath myself and then hump it outside, I used to feel as though I needed another bath by the time I'd finished – and it was easier by then as we had electricity and an electric copper.

Joan Hale

23

Letchmore Green between the two wars.

Wooding at Cuckoo Wood

I can remember the General Strike of 1926, not so much from the point of view of work because obviously I didn't start work until the '30s, but what I can remember was everyone was so short of coal and means of keeping warm that we used to go wooding. The nearest wooding place was Cuckoo Wood up on the other side of Rectory Lane. I suppose it's disappeared now, but we used to go up there and get the old wood – branches and things like that. I think it was a pram my mother used to fill with wood to bring home and saw up. Anyway we kept warm.

Walter Marchant

Coming into Paradise

I was born in 1920, at Hitchin, in the Mayflower Nursing Home, but my family lived in Letchmore Road on Letchmore Green. There's a new house built there now, we lived in the old house that was pulled down. I am the youngest of five children and we lived in Letchmore Road until I was, I think, about seven or nine and then we moved because the house was condemned. We had the chance of a new council house in Longcroft Road, well, after living in this very old house with an outside lavatory and sort of stable doors with big latches and winding stairs it was really lovely. I can always remember the smell of new wood which was absolutely wonderful, we thought we were going into paradise.

Dorothy Storton

The Beerhouse

Number eleven Trinity Road used to be a beerhouse. That was a house where they could serve beer only, they were not allowed to serve spirits and the houses were not public houses as we know them today. My Dad used to say when you went into one of the beerhouses, you went and sat in their front room and they brought the beer to you. The house at number eleven was known as Trussell's Beerhouse and I can remember the big cellar there and the very large bedrooms. You could get two double beds in each room.

E. Woods

We All Helped Each Other

If anyone was ill there was always someone there to look after you. Nobody was left on their own, to fend for themselves, they all helped each other, that was the good part of it. They hadn't got a lot, but you didn't need a lot, because it was love and friendship. You shared, if you'd got anything, you just shared it with each other, Christmas time especially. We all used to dress up and we used to go in each others' houses, just to say, 'Hullo!' and 'A Happy Christmas to you,' and have a little drink and then we'd go on to someone else's house, and by the time we'd finished, you'd got a trail of everyone behind you and it was gorgeous, you know. Nothing like today. The Christmases are nothing, are they, today?

Elsie Hills

I Can't Afford It

My father was always in work. He didn't get very much – two pounds fifty a week and you had to pay five shillings a week rent. We didn't have very much and my mother used to take in sewing. Often she'd have an old pair of men's trousers, and she'd cut them down to make little boys' trousers for certain people that were very poor. I won't mention any names, but sometimes I had to take them back to these parents and my mum would say, 'Now, be sure you get the money,' but often I didn't. They would say, 'I can't afford it.' So they were very poor and we were poor.

Lily Glazebrook

Kitchen Range

Living accommodation was confined to a small area. My mother, for a number of years, cooked on a kitchen range, heated by a solid fuel fire. This was in the same room where you ate, relaxed, and received visitors – usually cousins popping in.

Eventually she had a gas stove installed in the scullery and for a while was quite fearful of the contraption.

Roy Findley

Gooseberry Bushes

At home, we'd only got a little old yard, a plum tree and a little garden bit, but grannie had quite a big garden, she grew gooseberry bushes. My uncle Jim lived on the end. They were all family along that row, because my grannie's sister and her husband lived in the end cottage, so there were all family all around then. They kept rabbits, tame rabbits and they used to eat them. I don't think I would want to eat them if I'd kept them, not really. If I'd looked after them I don't think I could have eaten them.

Kathleen Jackson

Three Generations

My mother was born in that house, I was born in it and my daughter, Carole, was born in it. My grandad lived with us, my grandmother being dead and my family consisted of Mum, Dad, my brother, myself and Grandad at that time. My grandad was a farm bailiff. He worked for Marriotts and I still remember going down there every Sunday morning with him, to feed the horses and feed the chickens. I remember the huge amount of corn there was there. We used to scoop it up – I've still got the scoop that we used to feed the chickens then. And Grandad used to show horses – and very good, they were.

Louise Richards

Family portrait by the Stevenage photographer, Middleton, *c.* 1912. Back row, left to right: Florence Carter (later Mrs Joseph Johnson), Fred Carter, Arthur Carter, Alan Smith, Helen Carter. Front row: Sarah Carter, Thomas Carter, Eliza Carter.

Fairlands Farm, 1930s.

Everything We Wanted

Hutchinsons used to deliver our hot cross buns and doughnuts and they used to hang them on the handle on the doorstep. In Albert Street we didn't have to go out for anything. We'd got everything we wanted in Albert Street, even a chapel and two pubs.

Patricia Smith

Springfield Passage

We were six in the family, four boys and two girls. My eldest brother, Vic, got married when I was four years old and it was the first time I'd ever been out of Stevenage I think, when I went to Graveley where he got married. My brother George, he got married first and he moved into number one, Springfield Passage to get a house. It was adjoined to our house, that was next door. Eventually my brother moved further up Springfield Passage to number five where my grandfather and grandmother had lived.

E. Woods

300 Years in Shephall Parish

My father's family go back 300 years in Shephall parish, but I think they were all born, seven girls and one boy, in the Broadwater area. He lived in the last big house going out of Stevenage, Lytton House. He left there in 1900 and moved to near his sisters, Betsy and Charlotte, that lived in Trinity Road, and took the White Swan pub. He kept that as a pub, Grandad did, for twenty-five years. I know ours was the White Swan and next door was the Lord Roberts.

Roy Gates

Old cottages, Graveley, 1920s.

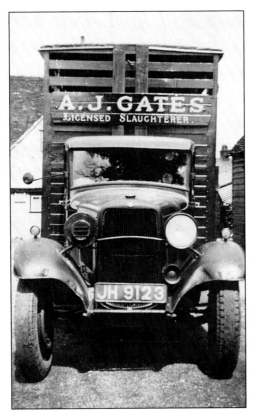

Gates' lorry, 1930s.

Paraffin to Chocolate

Our shop was a general store, selling everything from paraffin to chocolate. My father opened the shop about seven o'clock in the morning and would stay open until ten o'clock at night. On Sundays he would open until about one. I was an only child. I played with the neighbours' children and because my father and mother kept a shop, they could never afford to close it to go on holiday because when they came back the customers would have been going somewhere else. So I never went on holiday and when other kids were on holiday I sat on the kerb by the side of the road outside the shop, feeling sorry for myself because it would be a beautiful day and no one to play with.

Don Hills

Gaslight

Each room, except the middle bedroom, had gas lighting, which gave a soft mellow light. The middle bedroom was lit by a candle. It was also necessary to take a candle up the stairs as there was no lighting there.

Joan Hale

Lamp on a Pulley

I remember the oil lamp we used to have in Huntingdon Road – great big thing, used to come down on a pulley from the middle of the ceiling. You used to fill it up, light it, and then push it back up again. That was before the electric was brought in.

Roy Gates

Fish, Fruit and Coal

We lived at the grocer's shop at 65, Albert Street. Next door was the greengrocer's shop Mr Welch had, and the fish shop my grandfather had. My Dad had a coal business at the back. I was born in the house. My father's mother bought those three shops after the First World War. She came from Battersea, in London. She was granted a licence for a fish and chip shop because she'd got three sons coming out of the Army. She ran that shop with her sons and the fish shop is there now.

Patricia Smith

All in the Family

My grandfather, William Findley, had purchased the houses numbered 10 and 12 Albert Street. Later my father established the business of hairdresser and barber at number 10 and his brother John, a skilled carpenter and joiner, made umbrellas and did picture framing at number 12. At one time part of the premises of number 10 was used as a sweet shop. My other grandfather, Thomas Gray, a wood dealer, lived in a thatched cottage in the Twitchell and when this became uninhabitable he was brought to number 10, where he lived until his death at the age of ninety-five. His son, my mother's brother, had moved into number 62, Albert Street, which

Robert Gray with his mother in Trinity Road, late 1920s.

29

Advertisement for J. Findley, hairdresser and tobacconist, 1930s.

had once been The Black Swan public house, and carried on a wood dealer's business from there. An unusual feature of numbers 10 and 12 was internal access between the two because space had to be shared, as the gentlemen's barber shop was the front room of number 12, and the ladies' hairdresser's the front room of number 10. The umbrella and picture framing took place in the side room of number 12 and the sweet shop in the side room of number 10.

Roy Findley

Friday's Faggots

Friday night was the best night, when the faggots came up from Hutchinson's. They came up on a trades bike, with a great big metal tray and as soon as it went by the shop, you'd run up there with a basin. Everybody ran. Hutchinson's bakehouse – oh! I can smell it now.

Patricia Smith

Victorian House

Our house then was like Victorian days. There was no electricity there when we moved in. It took me about three months to make it so we could get married and go and live there. We lived there until it was compulsorily purchased, but it was as a Victorian house - coal ovens and fires and gas lighting.

Mrs Gates

The Sink in the Garden

In the scullery there was a shallow yellow sink with no stopper over the holes. An enamel bowl or oval zinc bath was placed in the sink. There was one cold tap over the sink; this was the only place where there was water inside the house. This old sink is now out in the garden with plants in it! Much later, after the 1939/45 war, we had a deep white sink with a plug-hole and plug which we thought was wonderful. In the 1960s we acquired a stainless steel sink unit which is a great joy.

Joan Hale

Hills Home Library

My sister, Joan, was born with a curvature of the spine and she'd got ribs missing. In this day and age they would have done something. She used to work in the little library, Hills Home Library it was, part of Deamer's shop now. She used to have a lot of nerve trouble and she died in 1953 when she was thirty-seven. My brother,

he was too young, he'd got no interest in the milk round. If I wanted a day off for anything, he didn't really like doing it. I never used to have a day off for Christmas or anything ... still you just took it in your stride, didn't you, and just did it.

Kathleen Jackson

All Publicans

Originally, my mother's mother took the White Horse on from the Buckingham Palace, in Middle Row. They were the first tenants in the White Horse, their name was Newberry. When Jack Newberry died, Grandma kept it on and then she passed it on to her son, another Jack Newberry. They

Joan Phipps, with her dog, Judy, at the door of the Hills Home Library, c. 1950.

31

were there during the war, then after they came out, it passed on to a cousin, Lionel Palmer. That was Grandma's brother's boy, they'd always had the Diamonds, all publicans. After that, Sid Jackson and Daphne took it over, and Daphne was a cousin to Mum, so it's been in the family quite a long time. Then a manager came.

Patricia Smith

Frozen Out

In 1956 the last little bit of building at the end of the Cromwell was owned privately. The ground floor was a welfare clinic and upstairs was the Nursing Officer's flat. It was a very, very cold flat because all the water pipes were outside so at a touch of frost everything froze up and usually burst as well. I was out from eight thirty to half past five or six, to come home to a freezing cold flat. I was there about eight years before I started looking for a house and eventually found one over in Symonds Green before that area developed at all. So with a thankful heart I moved out of the flat into my own little house.

Stella Kestin

The Longest Journey

We had to walk up as far as Grove Road to go to the toilet. Our garden went from Albert Street to Grove Road and our toilets were right on the end. We'd never got any water in the winter. They'd frozen up.

Patricia Smith

Newspaper Was Best

To get to the lavatory we went out of the back door and round to the back of the house. There was a flush cistern on the wall, with a chain. On the wall was a hook from which we hung newspaper torn into squares: a hole was made through one corner with a metal meat skewer and a piece of string threaded through and tied to hang it up. Newspaper was best, the *Radio Times* was too hard and shiny. Later on we had Izal toilet roll with rhymes advertising Izal (and disinfectant Sanizal) printed on it. I remember one:

> *Sing a song of sixpence*
> *Going down the drain*
> *Spent upon Sanizal*
> *That loss would have been gain.*

Joan Hale

Living on the Job

When I first was appointed to Barclay School the houses had not, of course, been built and so I said to Peter Osmund, 'Well, I really came to Stevenage because I've been married for ten years and we haven't had a home of our own.' He said, 'Well, I know that there is an allocation of educational houses but they've just used it up and you'll have to wait.' So I waited and he said, 'You can stay in the domestic science flat if you like.' So I said, 'Yes, OK, that's alright and I'll go home at weekends, then.' It was rather interesting, because the flat's right at the top of the Barclay School and if I got up fairly late I always had to shave

Peter Blagg aged about sixteen, with his parents in their garden at 88, Walkern Road.

lying on the ground because the pupils would come pouring in through the back entrance and if I stood up they could see their English teacher happily stripped to the waist shaving, so I always had to crouch on the ground to keep myself fairly invisible. It was fun though.

Robert McArthur

A Motley Collection

We lived at 88, Walkern Road, which was part of the first row of houses which were built for people who were going to be working in the New Town. My father was a builder – a carpenter and joiner. A motley collection of architects, quantity surveyors, draughtsmen and artisans were sent into these houses in the top part of Walkern Road, which went round opposite the green in Walkern Road and round the corner into Letchmore Road.

Peter Blagg

No Car Outside

My youngest son was born in 1961, at home, and I can remember the midwife saying, 'I can see you've got old fashioned parents,' and I said, 'How's that?' She said, 'Well you've got carpet on the floor and you've food in the larder but you haven't got any car standing outside.' So I said, 'We couldn't afford to run a car.' She said, 'No, lots of people can't but they still have one.'

Kate Cope

I Put Down Roots

When I came to Stevenage I had decided that I would come here for two years and then move on. At the end of two years all the towns, and the work, were growing at such speed, I was only just beginning to get a grip on what I was doing and I thought, 'Well, I'll stay another two years,' because I was enjoying life. At the end of four years I thought, 'Now, shall I move or shall I buy a house?' and the house won. So I stayed there and I stayed in the job until 1970. For the last two plus years I worked from County Hall and Welwyn Garden City. When I finally retired in 1972, I thought, 'No, I can't move now. I've put roots down, I've made friends. If I move I shall lose all that.' So I've no regrets at all about staying.

Stella Kestin

Cut Off

We didn't have a telephone and we used to have to walk down to the Roebuck, there was a telephone there and I can remember sitting my eldest son, who was my only child at the time, on the little ledge there and him putting his hand down on the telephone and cutting us off and then not having any change and having to go home again to get more change to come back and make the call again.

Kate Cope

Jumping for Joy

Eventually Catherine Carr said to me, 'Robert, there's a house going in Fairview Road, but you've only got until tonight to say whether you want to buy it or not.' I rang up my wife, who was still in Croydon, and she came up by train and we looked around 122, Fairview Road in darkness, striking matches to see what was going on. Clifford Carr, Catherine's husband, who weighed fifteen stone, I think, said, 'I'll jump up and down on the floorboards and see if it's got any dry rot.' So, there we were, jumping up and down in the house, looking round it with matches and of course we said we'd have it. We were absolutely desperate.

Robert McArthur

34

CHAPTER 3

Education

St Nicholas' Girls' School with the 'offices' (outside toilets) in the background. From the left: Marie Ward, -?-, -?-, Eileen Cherry, Faith Furnell, Nancy Lane, Betty Furr, Cynthia Upton, Mary Clarke, Monica Newberry.

My First Schoolteacher

St Nicholas Girls' School was on the Bury Mead, beside a wonderful avenue of trees, they were absolutely magic. In the spring there was the lovely greenery and in the autumn one walked up to one's knees in golden leaves and the rustle and the dust was really something. It was a wonderful walk. The first schoolteacher that one had – she was there for years – was a Miss Rogers and she was a marvellous, sporty type of person. She had choker pearls and big pearl ear-rings, short curly hair and she was a really outdoor type. She was a wonderful teacher and everybody loved her, so you went there for the first year.

Dorothy Storton

A Good Education

I went to school at the Infants' School down by the Bury Mead – St Nicholas infants school – and then I went to the boys' school in Letchmore Road, which is now an an infants' school in itself. For the fact that one finished school at fourteen years old, I think we had a very good education. I also think that the town was lucky in having a sixth-form master that really went out of his way to make life interesting for the children and I've never heard anyone who went to that school run him down or say a bad word about him. Cecil Clark his name was, and he came from Wheathampstead, and he was a marvellous man.

Walter Marchant

A Present for Everyone

Miss Woods ran the Grove Road school. I remember at that school Christmas was the great thing. There was a Christmas tree on the stage and there was a present on the tree for every child and Miss Woods would invite you

St Nicholas' School building on Bury Mead by the Avenue.

up on to the stage and give you your present, that was superb, that was great. I remember the hymns that we learned as a kid. 'All things bright and beautiful' was one of course and I think the first thing I ever learned to sing. If you were naughty as a boy then you had to sit down the front with the girls, that was the punishment. I'm sure in some mixed secondary schools today they might deliberately be naughty in order to sit there, but we certainly didn't. That was the biggest insult of the lot, to have to go and sit down the front with the girls.

Don Hills

A Very Severe Man

I went to St Nicholas' school, until I was of an age to go to the Boys' School in Letchmore Road and after that I went to Alleyne's Grammar School, until I left school in 1948. The head master was Mr H.P. Thorne, who had a year to go before his retirement, when I went there. He had been there since 1915. He was one of the old school, a very severe man but a very good headmaster.

Wilf Neilson

The Mystery of the Figure of Eight

Mrs East was a tall angular person with black hair and a fringe. She used to wear trim skirts and she was very strict. One particular instance – of course we had slates and chalks at that stage – we were doing numbers and she put them on the blackboard and we had to copy them on the slate and I copied the figure eight and she walked round and she said, 'What is that?' and I said I didn't know and she said, 'Give me your finger,' and she took my index finger and she said, 'Now you sit and do this until you know what it is.' The bell rang and it was playtime. They had a teachers' meeting at playtime and I still sat there doing this figure of eight and I dare not move and when she came back almost half an hour later she said, 'Oh, child, you're not still sitting there are you?' But of course I was. I'd been told to do it and one did that and my finger was really sore. I've never forgotten that and when I hear anybody say they are doing a figure of eight now I think, I know a figure of eight.

Dorothy Storton

Mr Roach, the Headmaster

I worked in Stevenage first of all in 1945, at Letchmore Road Boys' School. My name was Miss White then. The headmaster was Mr Roach. He had a sort of Victorian, chauvinistic attitude to women, 'You women,' he said, 'I treat you like little flowers.' I had to do a lot of chores which he should have been doing, but he did treat me like a flower in a way. I didn't have to do any playground duty, which was a great joy. I really didn't do much dinner duty, because I went with Mr Clark and I just stood about while he did all the roaring at the boys. Mr Roach's office was right opposite my classroom. His job seemed to be going round the classrooms doing mental arithmetic and getting a line of boys outside his door, which was always

Miss Joan White, a teacher at Letchmore Road boys' school, in 1945.

by computers but we used to have to work it all out in old coinage. I always remember the two hundred and forty pence to the pound, you know and four hundred and eighty halfpennies and nine hundred and sixty farthings, they told us how to work it out. Then, from there, when we were seven we went to the Letchmore Road Boys' School and there is when we started doing most of our education, learning mental arithmetic and also doing what they call cursive writing, when you join it up together. Mrs Davis used to teach us how to do all the cursive writing and when you had the cane off of her, she didn't hit you with the cane she hit you with a stick or with the leg of a chair.

E. Woods

preceded by, 'To my room!' I'd got seven year olds, little boys, so when he came in to do mental arithmetic with them, according to their temperaments, some of them went red with fear and some of them went white with fear. If they didn't get it right, or weren't quick enough, he tended to grind his teeth at them. But, my goodness, they were good at mental arithmetic. He certainly taught me how to teach mental arithmetic.

Joan Catteau

Hit With the Leg of a Chair

They used to call it arithmetic in those days. I don't know what they call it today because it's all done

Black Marks

You got black reports, you never got the cane. If you did anything wrong, you got a black mark and if you got three black reports you had to go before the headmistress. I never knew of anybody getting the cane. In those days, you respected the teachers, you daren't answer a teacher back, or anything like that. Times have altered, haven't they?

Mrs I. Cotts

We Swept the Board

Each year there was a Hitchin & District schools sports day held at Hitchin Football Ground with teams from Hitchin, Letchworth and Stevenage. A shield called the Francis Ransom trophy was competed for each year. In my and other fellow competitors' particular races we swept the board. George Welch, Jack Smith, myself and others whom I forget now, came first and later were entered for county sports which badge I still have. Afterwards on arriving home in Stevenage the teacher in charge took us into Mr Horsnell's sweet shop for a large lemonade.

Norman Palmer

Sports Days

At school I used to do a lot of running, I used to be a good runner and I did a lot of running for North Herts. We had Sports Days where, if you were good enough, you ran in the county. You had to qualify for it, you had to work your way up to it, and we used to train in the Avenue.

Mrs I. Cotts

Clean Bowled

At one point Mr Roach decided to have a staff versus boys cricket match. Actually, Miss Ashford had played cricket for Hertford Ladies' team. She was a good cricketer, she had all the equipment, great pads and so forth – I didn't. There was a boy called Briars. He was one of the oldest boys and those boys weren't very much younger than I was. All the staff had to have a turn in and when it came to my turn to bat, Briars was the bowler and Mr Roach said to him, 'Go easy on her, Briars,' So I went in and to their utter astonishment I scored straight away – thirteen runs! I got several boundaries, actually. Oh dear, oh dear. Then I heard

Letchmore Road Boys' School, early twentieth century.

him say, 'Get her out, Briars,' so I was bowled out then.

Joan Catteau

The School Centenary

Let me just tell you about the school centenary. I was one of the older girls selected to hold bowers of flowers. The bower was a bendy bit of wood and all the big houses had given flowers and we decorated them. I don't know whether we were Australia or Canada, but we had Wellington boots, riding breeches, white blouses, a kerchief and we borrowed a scout's wide hat which we cocked up at one side. Mary Salt and I held this bower. Well, of course the other girls had to wear white blouses with their clothes tucked into their navy knickers and they were saying, 'Hmm, we're not going to do that' – because the boys' school were going to have front seats you see – 'We're not going to march in front of them in our knickers.' But of course they had to and we said, 'It's alright for us, we've got these on, we're alright.' Then we all went up to the field that the grammar school had for their sports, beyond the Bury Mead and we sat on the grass and had tea and biscuits and lemonade and we were all given a mug with a picture of the school, 1834-1934 which I've got and it's absolutely just as I was given it and that's sixty-four years ago.

Dorothy Storton

Reluctant Strippers

I was trained that children take off as much as possible for PE. It's very difficult to get little boys to strip off. I've

St Nicholas' Girls' School parade through the High Street. In the background is Simpson's dray delivering to the Unicorn.

40

known little boys come into a class room on a boiling hot day with a pullover and a jacket on top, and you say, 'Take some of that off', they do it with great reluctance. Having been fresh out of college, you do the right thing, you put your college shorts on and you go outside. Now this caused an enormous sensation.

Joan Catteau

Sex Education

I always remember Mr Roach's sex education. He used to say, 'Boy, remember your mother was a girl once.' That's as far as he got.

Roy Findley

We Sat Three in a Desk

I really don't know how the girls and infants all got into St Nicholas' school buildings. But we did. And of course, during the war, we had to use church halls and then for part of the time we only had the school for half a day. Where evacuees came with schools, they used our school building. But the others, who came individually, they came with us. We used to sit three in a desk.

Joan Amis

You Do it My Way

Sometimes you did cookery, sometimes you did laundry. We went in an orderly crocodile to the tin hut in Stanmore Road. The benches were the

St Nicholas' school centenary mug.

ones the boys had for woodwork but of course they were cleaned down. You had to take your own ingredients and you had to take your own laundry and to this day I still fold table linen concertina fashion. I went there one day and we were doing laundry and we had these little mangles on stands and we got the washing out and I'd got this little teacloth. My mother would always put it through roughly to get the worst out then she would shake it and fold it and then put it through again, so I did this and the teacher was behind me and she said, 'Dorothy Newberry what do you think you are doing?' So I said, 'Well, my mother always does it this way.' She said, 'I'm sorry to disappoint you but you are here and you do it my way, the way you are being taught, never mind what your mother says, it's not your mother who's teaching it's me,' and you know, I've never forgotten that.

Dorothy Storton

St Nicholas' Girls' School pupils at the county camp at Cuffley in 1946. Back row, left to right: Joan Rumley, Doreen Hird, Stella Minnis(?), Doreen Sams, Delia Smith, Maureen Sharp. Front row: June Farrington, Shirley Watkiss, Joan Boorman, Margery Braybrook, Nancy Briars. At the back are the Cuffley Camp warden, and teacher Mrs Katherine Carr.

I Wouldn't Go

I went to the Girls' School in the Avenue from five years old until I left school. I was supposed to go to the Girls' Grammar School at Hitchin, but I wouldn't go, much to the disgust of my father. I didn't pass the scholarship, so Mum and Dad would have had to pay for me. But I wouldn't go because my friend, my lifelong school friend, she couldn't afford to go and she didn't pass the scholarship and because she couldn't go, I wouldn't go and it caused a great irruption in our house.

Louise Richards

The Eleven-plus Examination

I was at St Nicholas' School for three years – I can remember doing that funny knitting with cotton reels and using a slate – then after the third year we transferred to Letchmore Road Boys' School which, funnily enough, was built by the family. After two years I took this examination to go to Alleyne's Grammar School. I went to Alleyne's in 1944, September 20 was the actual day, and I was nine, six days later. I'd taken the entrance examination in March and I passed and went to the school with several others and we were at Alleyne's before the Education Act of the new Labour government. They brought in the eleven-plus exam. Having passed an examination to get there, I had to pass another one to stay there and it was a very

St Nicholas' School May Day celebrations, 1934/5.

worrying time. Some people had to leave the school.

John Austin

A Very New School

I was eventually called for interview to Barclay School, Stevenage, which was very, very new at that time. This was in 1950 and the school had been opened in 1949. The headmaster was Peter Osmund. I wandered up to the school through the Back Lane, not the Walkern Road way and I thought, 'This is a curious place to have a school,' and then suddenly the whole glory of Barclay School was exposed unto me – this incredible Henry Moore statue in the garden. It was unlike any school I'd ever seen in my life, it was so spacious. I got into the interview room and Peter Osmund and Phil Ireton, who

John Austin, aged ten, as a choirboy at Holy Trinity church, 1943.

43

Letchmore Road Boys' School gardens, early twentieth century.

was Chairman of the Council at the time, and Chairman of the Governors of Barclay School, interviewed me. I got the job, to be English Teacher in charge of the library, and the library was massive and the whole school was massive and in those days it was pristine and new.

Robert McArthur

A Wondrous, Magical Place

I started at Barclay School and found it a wondrous, magical place compared with the awful, dreadful multi-story, drab London school that I'd been to previously. The headmaster was Mr Osmund, my art teacher was Jean Ashworth, my craft teacher was Ron Braddock, my English teacher was his wife, Mrs Braddock and Mr Clark, otherwise known as Nobby, used to attempt to teach me mathematics, but failed miserably. Mr Pritchard used to teach us what was then called rural science, as it sounded a respectable way of teaching gardening. And that was where

I first learned to prune fruit bushes which occasionally I've found useful.

Peter Blagg

A Wry Sense of Humour

Mr Clark used to do selections from Handel's *Messiah*. He got the boys to sing it as well. 'Unto us a child is Born' and he used to bang away on the piano. He used to stand up when he played, which is a common device of teachers. He was a good teacher. The boys, I think, liked him very much. He had a sense of humour, a wry sense of humour. He was getting towards retirement when I knew him.

Joan Catteau

A Breadth of Vision

It was a totally new experience in education, to give these children a breadth of vision and a look into the

44

outside world and try to train them for post-war Britain, which was full of hope, a sort of feeling of hope and expectation at that time.

We were still desperately poor, of course, and not much to eat and all the rest of it and yet there was a great spirit of hope, I think, abroad. And so I was part of this experiment and Barclay School was one of the first secondary modern schools to be built in the county, purpose built for this new idea in education. The only trouble was the school leaving age was still, I believe, fifteen at the time, and in fact, when I went to Barclay School to begin with, if you got the fourth year, which they were called in those days, you either had 4C, 4E, or 4S – 4 Christmas, 4 Easter and 4 summer and believe you me, if you had a class of thirty-odd Christmas leavers, and you were entertaining them on Friday afternoon, it was not easy, not easy.

Robert McArthur

No Time to be Lonely

I think I was very lucky because the Barclay School was a very socially innovative kind of establishment. There was no time, really, to be lonely because there were so many things going on at the school. You couldn't fail to get involved with all members of the local community. People then were coming from all over the place, every village on the outskirts fed Barclay School and so there was a very good mix of people from both very, very rural parts of the area as well as the town itself, such as it was.

Peter Blagg

The Remedial Specialist

I was at Bedwell Junior from 1978–1982. By then I was not only the music specialist but also the remedial specialist. I went there because one third of the children were in need of special attention, so I had a third of the school every day, withdrawn for reading and number work. The problems there were recognized, so the children were more helped by the educational system in the 1970s.

Joan Catteau

County Badge Scheme

I remember taking part in the County Badge Scheme at school, and I chose art for my project. Miss Lawrence, the headmistress, arranged for me to go and see Mabel Culley one Saturday morning so I went to her house and showed her what I had done and she and her sister were very, very kind. They were lovely ladies. a bit old-fashioned as I remember, but very, very kind, and she criticised the work quite kindly and pointed out the mistakes and she also gave me a postcard of one of her drawings.

Joan Amis

The Artist's Studio

Mabel Culley got interested in me and offered me the use of her studio, which was a large wooden shed. I'm guessing that she was probably around her early seventies at the time. She had this wooden studio and whoever put it together didn't do it that well,

Barclay School performance of *Alice* produced by Robert McArthur. Peter Blagg is the King of Hearts, seated on his throne next to the queen, *c.* 1952.

because there were big patches of daylight between all the boards. I remember being in there one day when it was rather cold, with this paraffin stove going like mad and the wind was blowing through and it made absolutely no difference at all, except when the wind dropped the smoke from the paraffin stove filled the place and I emerged completely blackened by the experience.

Peter Blagg

A Mixture of Cultures

But it was very difficult when the New Town children came in, because you began to get an influx and a mixture of cultures then. Not that they were disobedient at all. Many of these families came into this paradise, for them. They had a house and a garden and for many of the children it was unbelievably wonderful. But, of course, they brought London ideas and these clashed with Stevenage ideas and there was quite a lot of difficulty in handling a class of mixed children at that time. Discipline was difficult because we were dealing with two different cultures, but many of the kids were anxious to learn and I don't think the Old Town people resented the new people coming. I can't remember that feeling at all.

Robert McArthur

Night School

When I left school, I worked at the HRD, in the office. The factory was at Fishers Green and the offices were at the top of the High Street, near the Grange. I went to night school to

46

Back garden of 88, Walkern Road under snow, 5 January, 1955. Painting by Peter Blagg.

learn shorthand, at the Boys' School in Letchmore Road. I learnt shorthand there and they taught me typing in the office.

Louise Richards

A Bad Start

I think art was the only thing I was any good at. By the time I came to leave school, having had a rather bad start in education in London, being wrapped up in the mix of eleven-plus failures, I felt it was really a last chance when I came to Stevenage. At that age it sounds ridiculous, but academically it looked very, very bleak for me. I think that Jean Ashworth was very supportive of me and made sure that I got in touch with the right kind of further education.

Peter Blagg

Robert McArthur.

47

Betty Game at her Open University graduation ceremony in Cambridge.

A Working Mother

My husband went to evening classes. I went to college in the afternoons to learn typing and computer skills. Once the children had got to grammar school age, I could get a job, but I still worked for an agency, so that I could be at home for the school holidays. It wasn't the thing then to leave your children.

Barbara Burley

Further Education

I took all my A levels at evening classes at the college. I knew the children were growing up and I wanted

a proper job. By then my parents had moved here. My mother was alive when I first started studying, then when she died, Dad sat with the children. I passed English and history, but I didn't finish sociology. Then I thought about teacher training, but decided against it. I eventually got a job as library assistant in the town centre, but again, I decided not to go on to study librarianship. Part of my job was to read stories to children in the Knebworth and Old Town libraries.

Patricia Palmer

Our Introduction to Books

Mr Badell introduced us to library books. On Friday afternoons he used to open up these boxes and there was a choice of books. But prior to that he used to read to us. We had *Alan Quartermain*, *King Solomon's Mines*, *The Thirty-nine Steps* and what have you and it led many lads into the library itself.

Roy Findley

Never Too Late

Soon after I started at St Nicholas' school I caught whooping cough, which developed into double pneumonia. For most of my schooldays I suffered with croup which severely affected my school attendance. But I loved reading and read widely all my life and at fifty-six years of age, after six years of study, I received my BA degree from the Open University.

Betty Game

CHAPTER 4

Work

Stevenage workers at a Second World War rally near the paddling pool in Letchworth.

Trouble-Maker

I left school at Christmas. Now, I was a bit of a bad boy, in other words I was insubordinate, to a foreman. I had better explain this a bit better. I went to the ESA, where everyone went, almost, after leaving school, and my job was a shop boy. Now the shop boy, from the carpenters' shop, had a very large truck and the job was to get stuff from the machine shop and take it up to the carpenters' shop. For some reason or other they decided to put the carpenters on to bonus. Well that was fine, but they went mad. I've seen perspiration actually falling off people because they worked so hard to get this extra halfpenny or what ever it was, but what happened was, instead of us taking say eight loads up per day we were taking twelve or fourteen loads. The shop boys had a meeting – there was no Union or anything of that – and I was elected. So I went up to Frank Barker, who was sort of liaison between the carpenters and the management, and politely said that as we were doing that much extra work could we not be included in the bonus scheme, and Frank Barker was quite a decent man – he said, 'I'll take it up to the management.' The next morning I took my truck down to the machine shop and the foreman of the machine shop came across with a dowel rod and said, 'I'll put this across your back. You're the trouble maker.' And me, being me, said, 'Well, I'm sorry Mr — but if you hit me with that you will also suffer,' and I won't say what I said I'd do to him! So within twenty minutes I got my cards and I was over the bridge, which was the railway bridge by the old station. This shows you how it was in those days. Well, I knew a man, a Mr Burrows, who used to do all the electrical installations for the North Met. He was a sub-contractor, they didn't have their own electricians, they hadn't got enough work, so I went to see him and he said, 'Oh yes, I'll give you a job, boy. If you're no good within a fortnight, you'll have to go.' I said, 'Well, that's fair enough'. That night, the so-called Mr —, called round to Mr Burrows and said, 'Don't employ him, he's a trouble maker,' and Mr Burrows said, 'I've known him all my life. I promised him a job for a fortnight and if he's any good I shall keep him and if he's no good he'll have to go.' And I was there for twenty three years.

Walter Marchant

Unpunctuality Was Not Tolerated

Dad always came home to dinner at mid-day. The factory had a hooter (which was quite a feature of pre-war Stevenage) which sounded at starting and finishing times. Unpunctuality was not tolerated. In the 1930s work was scarce and Dad was often on short time. Mum used to worry in case he got 'laid off' and he was very fortunate that he never was.

Joan Hale

A Little Bit of Perks

On the whole I think we were treated very well. When we first started there was no clocking

50

ESA cricket team, probably 1940s. The groundsman on the left is Leonard Palmer.

in or clocking out, all we had was a Westminster chimes clock on the table and that was that. When I started I think I was on about 35/- or something, but the point was, you see, we did get a little bit of perks. We were working on brass, so what we used to do, we used to keep all the swarf, all the brass swarf, as clean as we could. Then we used to put it in sacks, then Larkins of Biggleswade would come. Whoever was deputed to put their bike on the lorry would go to Biggleswade with the load, they'd weigh it, you'd go to the office, see Mr Larkin, he'd give you about £50 to £60, then you'd ride back from Biggleswade with the cash, and we used to have a share out when you got back. That was the perks. Oh, yes, it was approved by the management.

Arthur Cotts

Market Day

We took the cattle to Hitchin market and people used to say years ago that the roads were so crooked because there was no way of taking cattle to market unless you took them where they wanted to go. They'd go round trees and walk on the soft ground and that is why Walkern Road and other roads are so crooked. My father used to go to the Cock Hotel in Hitchin. There was a Corn Exchange nearby where corn was sold and that was where you met all the dealers. But people in those days were so honest. If you made a bargain that was it, they'd never change and run back. And also the men in those days that worked for us, they'd be laughing nearly all the day. The things they would say, not to

51

make me laugh, but just ordinary talk, I used to burst out laughing.

Stanley Marriott

The Wind-up Pumps

When I left school, Mr William Game said Mr Clark had given him my name as somebody who wanted a job, and he came up and saw me and said would I like to work for him. And so I started down there on 1st January 1933 at 7/6d a week and after a month I went up to 10/-. I didn't do anything with cars. I was in the office, serving

Connie Kilby (left) and Elsie Minnis leaving their work at the Stevenage Knitting Company, Sish Lane, 1936.

petrol, sweeping up, painting, making myself useful. This was when they had the old petrol pumps out the front and you had to wind them up. When I started petrol was about 1/2 or 1/3 a gallon. I had to be good at figures because I did all the money side of it. You used to have a till roll and add up all the pounds, shillings and pence. I would still do that now. I hate this old metric thing.

John Walker

The Job Wasn't For Me

When I left school I worked at the Knitting Company. I was fourteen. When I first went there I used to be stitching the garments together, we had to do it all by hand and then I went from there to pressing the woollens. Then from there I went to doing the wool on the machine. In that Knitting Company, you had only just one long room, and then up at the end was like a stage part and the governor, he sat up there at his desk so he could see you. He was watching. There must have been about thirty of us. I got 7/6 a week. That was six days a week, from eight until five and Saturday mornings we had to work. I think we only got a week for our annual holiday. It was quite interesting, but I left because I wanted more money and a friend of mine worked at the Spirella, at Letchworth. I was only there a week because all I was doing was cutting ends off of brassieres and I didn't like it, having worked in a small place for years, I couldn't settle down, not to sit there in a great big room. It wasn't for me.

Mrs I. Cotts

A Bike for £2 10s

I used to go home to lunch. I remember Mr Game let me have a bike, because we dealt with a firm named East London Rubber Company, Great Eastern Street, London. They used to supply not only motor car bits, but everything, bikes and tyres and batteries and everything, and he let me have a bike for £2 10s and I paid him off at half-a-crown a week.

John Walker

I Got Housemaid's Knee

When I left school, which was at about sixteen and a half, I decided to be a nursery nurse and my first job was with a Mr and Mrs Seebohm who lived at Toddington in Bedfordshire. My salary was £26 a year. I did receive my working clothes, which were a nanny's dress and aprons, and full board and lodgings and one half day off a week and one whole day off a month. I worked from about seven in the morning until the children went to sleep at night. Well, as I was the only nursery nurse – nursery maid they were called in those days – I had to do all the donkey work, shall we say, like get up in time to light a coal fire, scrub or wash everyday the nursery floor, make the cots up for the children, wait on the nanny, perhaps do the cleaning and the dusting in the nursery and at lunch time go to the kitchen and fetch the lunch. There was the nanny and there was a four year old, I think and a two year old and myself for lunch. I had to wash up afterwards, go for a walk in the afternoon with the children and then, at five o'clock in those days the children were put in what we would call their Sunday best to go to the drawing room to meet their Mum. The Nanny went down too, and then the children had their tea, after that they were bathed and put to bed. Nanny slept in the same room as the children so if they woke up in the night she saw to them, but if Nanny wasn't there I took over. I think I started in the February and then through kneeling and scrubbing the floor without anything under my knees, I got housemaid's knee so I had to pack it up and come home. I was there about eleven months.

Enid Bates

Back-breaking

If I told you I've carried hundreds of tons on my back you'd never believe me would you? Well, a sack of wheat was two hundredweight and a quarter. They were stacked two high in the sheds and father would say, 'There's a lorry over there, go and load it up.' You'd got to carry it through the sheds and when you got to the lorry, you couldn't reach high enough, so we had a railway sleeper. With two and a quarter hundredweight on your back you'd got to get up it and put the sack on the lorry. When you'd put twenty-five or thirty up there the driver would say, 'Jump up and give us a hand.' No one would do it today, they wouldn't lift a hundredweight. That was two hundredweight and a quarter. There were no fork lifts then.

Stanley Marriott

The Cross family and workers harvesting at Trotts Hill, 1930s.

Idyllic Days

Looking back, I think they were idyllic days at Aston House. OK, in terms of office accommodation, in terms of what people have now one might say they were grotty but one was working in a village and in very pleasant surroundings with tennis courts, where staff could play tennis in their lunch hour. Some of us played cricket on the cricket square. We had our own canteen. If we didn't want the canteen there were two pubs in the village where you could get your bangers and mash. We were ferried up to Aston House by Sworder's Coaches. But I can see the sense that one day it was sensible that if you were developing a New Town and expecting people to come and work and live in your office blocks, that you should set an example and be there first.

Alan Cudmore

When the Slaughtering Stopped

The slaughter house started where Boorman's yard was, back of the Coach and Horses. They say it had been going a hundred years when I was about here, so that would have been the 1850s, or something like that, but then they transferred it up to the yard of the White Swan pub and that was closed in 1972. The slaughter house wasn't actually owned by the White Swan, it was a separate business. It was my father's and grandfather's business. There was a farm as well, he had eight acres of ground, which the Development Corporation took. There were several fields there, one little one by the railway and there was one that they called Leg End which came down to the back of the Chequers and then there was one behind our house.

Roy Gates

Speed Impossible

The HRD was still making the motor bikes then all hand-assembled and pushed into other stables. It wasn't very high-tec. Everything was hand made there. They used to trundle the bikes out and then go off up the North Road to Letchworth Gate to do their trials and then come back. George Brown, I think, held the record, he was clocked at 119 mph, going through Graveley. He denied it. The judge said, 'Well, that's impossible, so I agree with you, sir,' and so he got off.

Wilf Neilson

I Worked for Dad

When I left school I just worked for Dad. All I ever did was help him. I used to go round on my bike before I

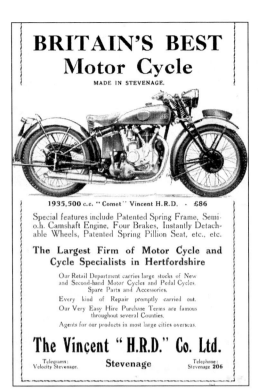

Advertisement for Vincent HRD motor bicycles.

Visit of government minister, Sir Stafford Cripps, to the HRD canteen, 1940s.

went to school and then leave my bike at home about nine, when we got back to Albert Street. And I used to be on the cart with Dad.

Kathleen Jackson

Stop For the Cars

In the summer we used to have the doors open and have a game of cricket. We'd get back to work early after lunch and a man would be right at the bottom of the garage, with a bat, a man on the front bowling and another chap in the middle of the road and another man, long stop, over near Harry James' farm house, Southend Farm. There wasn't much traffic then, because they'd bowl and the chap in the middle of the road would say, 'Oops, hold on a minute, I think there's a car coming.'

John Walker

Advertisement for Ibcol, 1946.

The Wicked City

When I finished my formal education, at seventeen, I wanted to be an accountant and my father got me a job with Price Waterhouse in London. Before I started there, however, my father went to a beekeeping meeting and met Mr Brignall, a local solicitor, who told my father that he needed a new clerk in his Stevenage office. My father thought it would be much better for me to work locally and not to have to go up to the wicked city every day and so I finished up, quite happily, working with Mr Brignall and a senior clerk. Mr Brignall was a lovely, old, eccentric gentleman, a Shavian character, with some peculiar traits. For example, he used to change into a thinner suit on the first of April no matter what the weather was like and changed into a thicker suit on the first of October even if it was sunny and hot.

Eileen Harding

You Could Tell by the Smell

Up the North Road we had Ibbetson's, the Ibcol factory, that used to make the disinfectant and things like that. It was all very interesting. When we used to go to dances, you could always tell a girl that worked at Ibcol's by the smell of carbolic.

Wilf Neilson

Penny-farthing a Line

The *Hertfordshire Express* only had eight pages in those days and one of those, of course, was the front page which was taken up entirely with adverts. There were adverts obviously on other pages so the amount of news columns was not very high. Every village had its correspondent, who was paid about a penny farthing a line for what was published.

Don Hills

No Annual Rises

At my interview with Mr Brignall he offered me £1 a week and this was in April 1930. I told him of my training and qualifications (I had sixty words a minute typing and one hundred and twenty words a minute shorthand) and I was then offered £1 10s 0d and started work at that salary. You didn't get rises annually at that time, you waited until it was thought your work was improving and then you'd get, perhaps, a half a crown rise and that's the way it was done – nothing was taken for granted. When I was married in 1938 I was getting £3 15s 0d and at the same time my husband was paid only £4 0s 0d although he was a qualified chemist.

Eileen Harding

Freedom is Ahead

In 1956, I got appointed to North Herts as Divisional Nursing Officer. Stevenage at that time came into North Herts so I had an enormous area to cover, supervising district nurses, district midwives, health visitors, nursing homes, day nurseries, child-minders and anything else that needed doing. I started with thirty-three staff and by the time I retired in 1970 I had over ninety, so the whole area grew alarmingly fast and it got almost unmanageable single handed. After I retired, nine people took my job, so I wasn't surprised that I had felt over-worked. But I had no regrets at all. I retired early at fifty-five because my mother was ill and actually she died before my date of retirement came and I was offered my job back, but I thought, 'No! Freedom is ahead,' and so I've enjoyed a very busy retirement ever since 1972.

Stella Kestin

BBC Sporting Quiz

I left the *Express* (by then called the *Gazette*) on 31st December 1959 and I joined the Development Corporation the next day. My first job was press relations with the Development Corporation and producing the quarterly magazine *Purpose* and also I was given the job then of training two teams from Stevenage to take part in the BBC New Towns Sporting Quiz. That was great fun and Stevenage finished as finalists and were pipped at the post by one point.

Don Hills

The Largest Doors in the World

When I first started working in the office at the ESA, I was in what they called the planning office. They were making the large hangar doors for

The old Stevenage railway station at the top of Julian's Road.

the Brabazon hangar and that was the largest door in the world and then they started making the hangar doors for Heathrow.

Enid Bates

Peppermint Time

Where the Catholic church, St Joseph's, is now, near the farm, that used to be the horse meadow. One of the horse keepers – of course, he used to love his horses – and they'd be right down one end and he'd stand up the other end and he'd call out, 'Peppermint time,' and the horse would prick his ears up and he'd gallop right up to him. He used to give them them very strong, white peppermints. Of course, we used to breed our own horses and break them in in the early days.

Stanley Marriott

Tragic Air Crash

After I'd worked in Stevenage for about three months Mr Brignall said that his manager at Knebworth, Godfrey White, needed a clerk and would I like to go there. So for several years I worked at Knebworth. Mostly I went by train. I can remember coming out of Knebworth station one morning and there was a deadly hush in the town. I have never known anything like it. It was like a pall all over the village and I didn't know what had happened. I enquired and apparently Lord Lytton's son, Lord Knebworth, had been killed in an air crash. I think that must have been in the early thirties.

Eileen Harding

58

Flying the Flag

The flagpole outside the garage has got a Standard Vanguard piston on the top. It was put there when one of the mechanics made the flagpole and they wanted something to put up and someone suggested a piston, being as we were a garage. Being royalists, we put the flag up for high days and holidays.

John Walker

Murder, It Really Was

After the war, we just carried on. We got more advanced. You can just imagine the work when you had to cut round with a scythe round every field before you started. Murder it really was. You wouldn't pull thistles out of your arms because they were bleeding all day long so you had to keep on going, but then I enjoyed it. I loved the animals, I could do anything with them. I remember (after the new town came) Sybil was up at the school at Bedwell and we used to have the children down and I used to teach them about farming;

Gordon Johnson with a scythe at Trotts Hill.

chickens, pigs and all the lot and they went to Hertford and they took the first prize.

Stanley Marriott

CHAPTER 5

Health and Welfare

Dr B. Lyndon Skeggs with Red Cross Nurses. Back row, left to right: Miss Foster, Mrs W. Ivory, -?-, Miss O. Newey, -?-, -?-, -?-, -?-. Middle row: -?-, -?-, Miss Phillips, -?-, -?-, Miss Phillips, -?-, -?, Miss Morgan Smith. Front row: -?-, Mrs Smith, -?-, Dr Skeggs, -?-, -?-, Mrs Dorothy Griffith.

Her Little Black Box

At the bottom of Grove Road there lived one, Nurse Holmes, who was the District Nurse. Later on, instead of the bicycle on which she used to go round with her black box on the back, she had a little Austin 7, a little ruby saloon, which we thought was real progress then. But she was very nice and she did deliver most of the babies in Stevenage at that time.

Wilf Neilson

A Car for £200

We all had the choice of receiving a mileage allowance or we could borrow a County Council car and not use it for leisure. I preferred to have my own because of visiting the family. It was a Ford Popular. It cost just over £200 new. When I came here the Ford agent was Shelford and Crowe, in the High Street. Two brothers ran it, the Tucker-Peakes, and they looked after me very, very well, they took me under their wing. Now I go to Game's and they look after me well there too.

Stella Kestin

Birth Places

In the 1930s the nearest hospital was at Hitchin. My three children were born in the old Maternity Hospital, that was in Brand Street and further up was the old Lister Hospital which was actually developed during the Second World War years, and that is where the hospital in Stevenage eventually got its name.

Another hospital used by Stevenage people was Hertford. My father, he finished up in Hertford Hospital, back in the mid 1930s.

Roy Findley

All Home Births

It was all home births, unless there were complications and they had to go to hospital. The maternity unit was, of course, in Hitchin at that time. They were kept in for a reasonable length of time before being sent home. It wasn't a case of 'Born today – Home tonight.'

Stella Kestin

Never Coming Back

I had my adenoids removed when I was about six. I went to Hertford Hospital and it was absolutely horrible. I was terrified, and there were three older boys in the ward who tormented us like anything. I had a little boy next to me. I know that one of the older boys came from a children's home or something and he said our mothers were never coming back. After about three days I began to think this was probably true. It was awful. They really weren't very kind or thoughtful in those days.

Joan Amis

Easier on a Bike

I had my own car. I needed it to get from Knebworth to Royston and all

Shelford and Crowe's garage.

the villages in between, but quite a few of the staff were still on bicycles (mainly the part-timers) In some ways it was easier, especially as the New Town grew, because of the wonderful way of numbering houses and it was easier if you were getting hopelessly lost to push a bike than try to park a car.

Stella Kestin

A Brave Man

My husband was not called up in the war. To start with he was exempt because of being a chemist, but then he became seriously ill with a vascular disease, Thrombo Angitis Obliterans which could have killed him at any time. It was necessary for him to have a sedentary job and to leave his employment with Boots. He eventually found a very worthwhile job with Roche Products at Welwyn Garden City. In 1945 he had a leg amputated and we got a car for him with a special appliance for changing gear which was made by Shelford and Crowe, a garage in the High Street. Roche Products were very good to him, paying his salary regardless of his having to be away from work frequently and for long periods. He eventually had his other leg amputated. He was so brave and cheerful, in spite of terrible pain, and was without complaint. Bill was very interested in the Lytton Club and was a founder member of the Lytton Players for whom, in spite of his disability he painted scenery, hopping around on one leg! He was, for some time, chairman of the Youth Club.

Eileen Harding

Doctors

When I moved to Stevenage with my parents in 1935 I suppose there were only about 5,000 people in Stevenage. Our doctor was Dr Lyndon Skeggs and their practice (until they moved to Stanmore Road) was next to the old post office in the Old Town. I seem to remember that the school doctor at the time was Dr Grosvenor, who lived at The Poplars at the top of the High Street, and until fairly recently his only daughter, Dorothy Grosvenor, lived there and used to bike around. She was very much a local character. There were other doctors, there was Dr Swayne, and his wife, Dr Margaret Swayne.

Wilf Neilson

See Through

You had an Elsan toilet in the barn and there was more daylight coming through than woodwork. We all had to take a turn each digging a trench and cleaning the Elsan. That was the general rule.

Arthur Cotts

The Treat

In those days, nobody had indoor loos or bathrooms, only the very well-off. We used to think it was wonderful when we could go into a house down London Road, where my aunt worked in service and go into the toilet and pull the chain.

Lily Glazebrook

Bill and Eileen Harding, mid-1960s.

The Grange School, early twentieth century.

We Had to Take the Window Out

I can remember going to Springfield passage with my father in the early 1950s. A rather large-sized man had died upstairs in one of the cottages and the only way we could get him down was to put a ladder up and take the window out. He was a very big guy and we had to put him in a coffin and lower him down a plank on to the back of our lorry and it was a job getting the actual vehicle into Springfield Passage.

John Austin

Terrified

The doctor had a dispenser at the surgery who made up the prescription. Most of the medicines were liquid in bottles and they nearly all tasted basically the same, with some horrible ingredient. None of them were very nice to take. The surgery was not a very cheerful place, that I do know. It was dull and depressing. It terrified me, it was so gloomy and you had to sit there and be quiet, of course, which is so different today, and by the time I got in I was shaking. I know I was absolutely terrified. They didn't do anything to try and put you at your ease, either, and he just sat there like God himself.

Joan Amis

We Were Rather Frightened

I think my granny helped Mr Toll with what they called 'the laying out.' She was a strong-minded person, nothing seemed to frighten her and sometimes she used to come round to see my Mum and Dad and tell us all about these people she'd been sitting up with and sometimes, as children, we were rather frightened.

Lily Glazebrook

Laying Out

Dad built the first chapel-of-rest Austins ever had, in Letchmore Road back at the end of the Second World War. Before that, when someone died, we used to go out to the house and dad would say to me, 'Get on your bike and go up to number 40, Alleyn's Road and ask Mrs Mobbs if she'd go to So-and-So, or Mrs Ellis, or Mrs Haggar or Mrs Searle. There were four or five of them and these ladies would go out and do the necessary, wash the body, lay the body out, do the necessary plugging that had to be done and invariably tie the chin up and tie the ankles together, which was really not necessary, but that is the way it was done. Then, at night the next evening, or the same evening, you would take the coffin and you would then place the body in the coffin, lay it out and leave the coffin in the house until he day of the funeral.

John Austin

Lost Child

When my third son was being born we couldn't find the eldest one, and I was deeply in labour having the baby at home. He was down in what they called The Canyon and my husband had to hike him back, 'Get to bed while your mother has this baby.'

Kate Cope

W. Austin & Son, Builder & Undertaker, Letchmore Green.

Epidemics

I remember two girls from one family who had scarlet fever and one of them had her head shaved and obviously sent to an isolation hospital. I would think that there were so many people ill at times, that they used to go to Hertford. When I was at school, there was a whooping cough epidemic and a number of mothers who used to bring a pram didn't bring it any more. So obviously young children had died. Whooping Cough was one of the biggest killers, I think.

Joan Amis

Isolation Hospital

I remember scarlet fever and diphtheria being quite rife at school when I was perhaps about seven, at St Nicholas' school, and one girl in my class died from diphtheria. I had scarlet fever when I was three, and I went to an isolation hospital at Hertford and I was there for six weeks, and no one was allowed to visit me. You couldn't see your parents in all that time, and at three years old that was a bit disastrous.

Joan Hale

Home Deliveries

I couldn't understand why they built this town, and encouraged all these people to come, with no hospital. We had to have our babies at home. In London they would have been born in hospital. The midwifery service was excellent and the doctors very good. When I actually had the baby they were great. This was long before husbands could be present at the birth, but they let my husband be there.

Barbara Burley

Joan and Joyce Boorman, in their grandparents' garden at 31, Julian's Road.

New House – New Baby

Most of the work in Stevenage in the early 1960s was midwifery. People were pouring into the town and 'New house – New baby'. We had three full-time and two part-time midwives, and one full-time district nurse and because the age-range of the people was young there wasn't as much demand for nursing as there was for midwifery. I think it was in the early 1960s that Stevenage records show that we had twice the national birth rate. That is, reckoned per thousand of the population, our birth rate was very, very high and then it settled.

Stella Kestin

Hospital Fund

When I had my adenoids removed it was before the National Health Service. My father paid, I know, but he probably paid into the Hospital Fund. Nearly everybody did here. And there was a Hospital Saturday. I'm not quite sure how it worked, I was too young to take it all in. But I know my father did pay for the operation. We weren't wealthy but some relatives were and my aunt took me to hospital in the car.

Joan Amis

Registration Office

The Registration Office for this area was always at Hitchin, then they decided to bring a registrar into Stevenage, in the town centre, next to

Joan Boorman, with her aunt, Doris Belgrove, in the garden of her grandparents' house, 31, Julian's Road.

the library. Later it moved to the Grange, in the High Street, where they also introduced a room for weddings. The registration of births, deaths and marriages was on the right side of the archway and on the left was a fairly original part of the building, which had never been altered and was never really in very good shape. We were doing some building work for Herts County Council at the time and I asked if they needed those downstairs rooms. When we opened them up we found they'd still got the original hay-mangers and stalls for the horses and this was in the 1970s. The Divisional Education Officer agreed that we could do it, so we put our funeral office there and we stayed there until a few years ago.

John Austin

Clinics Were Popping Up

We had the yard behind the Clinic building for car parking and luckily it was very near to the end of Basil's Road where the Fire and Ambulance station was. So when the cellar at 27, High Street got flooded, I only had to nip up the road and ask the firemen to come and pump it out, which was quite frequent in winter time. It was used as a clinic until the owner died and the Cromwell bought it, and the clinic then moved to 'Glencoe,' the first house on the right in Julians Road, for quite a few years. In the meantime the Principal Health Centre, down in Southgate, was being built. There was another clinic attached to Peartree Infants' School and other clinics were starting to pop up over the town. We had a periodic one in St Andrew's church, another in St Peter's church and eventually one up in Camps Hill.

Stella Kestin

Stella Kestin, Divisional Nursing Officer, North Herts. with Dr V.R. Walker at the Divisional Health Office, Brand Street, Hitchin, 1958. (Courtesy *Nursing Times* and *Nursing Mirror*)

CHAPTER 6

Country Town

Trotts Hill Farm, mid-1950s.

The Skylark's Song

My chief memory of Stevenage is the fact that it was a rural town more than an urban town. I don't know the last time a lark sang in Stevenage, but when I was a youngster, I used to go up with my grandfather to the allotments which were up at the top of Walkern Road, number 99, and invariably from spring the larks used to rise up from the allotment and it was just beautiful. The other thing from my early memories was finding a lark's nest up the cart-way, when we went up to the allotments, with four eggs. To me it was a magical thing, something we'll never see here again.

Walter Marchant

Trotts Hill and Pin Green water tower, 1956.

Hob-nailed Boots

I can remember Mr Allison who made and sold harness: you went up three or four steps to his shop, but particularly I can remember Mr Titmuss's shop farther down. He also sold harness and when we were at school we heard that he was selling Wellington boots. At that time of day we always had to wear buttoned-up boots of leather, or shoes, and they never kept the rain out, so my mother took us to Mr Titmuss, my sister and I. There was a bell on the door and we seemed to have to walk quite a way to the counter. The Wellingtons were brown and he had a little stool, where we fitted them on and came home. I can't remember the price of them. I think he also sold hob-nailed boots for boys. In those days, poorer children always wore hob-nailed boots and he sold tips and studs that they could put on the shoes they already had.

Lily Glazebrook

Absolute Magic

We used to go down a long lane with high hedges and the birds would be singing and it was something that I don't think anyone would experience today. It was absolute magic and one would walk into the house and knock on the door and Mr Cope would be bringing the cows home and you'd hear the 'flip, flop' and they used to come across a rustic bridge and this was sheer magic for a child. 'Flip, flop' and he'd say, 'Coom on, coom on,' and he'd bring them home to milk.

Dorothy Storton

Clever Horse

Our milk was delivered by Mr Phipps, from number two, Albert Street, from his milk cart carrying the large urn from which he poured milk into a measuring jug of one pint or a quart and then into the customer's jug. People out to work would have a bottle left on their doorstep. The horse knew the route so well, that it anticipated the starts and stops, when to break into a trot and when it was heading for home. Some stops meant a titbit from the occupant of the house and one such stop was at Mr Fletcher's where it received a mixture of bread and treacle.

Roy Findley

Preservation Order

I was born in Trinity Road and grew up there. There were some very old properties in Trinity Road. A lot of them shouldn't have been pulled down. When they got to the end of the road, at what we call the old London Road now, there was a house there that they started pulling down and then they realised that there was a preservation order put on it, so they had to stop and start building it again as best as they could, but it's not the same as it was. Mrs Piggott used to live in that house.

There were about six cottages and then my house, where my mum and dad lived, was next and there was this great open space where the Stevenage Motor Company used to park all their cars. There was a well there, too and when we were kids we used to stand over this well and drop stones down to see how

Mr Phipps (left) with his horse.

far down it was. I often wonder now, with all the traffic that's going over that spot now, how they've managed to seal it all off.

Elsie Hills

The Muffin Man

There was not a lot of traffic up Trinity Road. The only traffic you got was traders coming up there, with a horse and cart, I can remember and then they changed over, the butcher and the milkman used to come round in vans and the muffin man used to come round Sunday afternoons. I don't know if you can remember those old

square box, three-wheeled carts that sold Wall's ice cream, well he had a similar thing to that. He always rung a bell. About three o'clock on a Sunday afternoon he'd come round shouting, 'Muffins.'

E. Woods

No Cars in the Street

There were a lot of horses and carts and bikes. If you had a car you were somebody, then. It was a small place in those days because you could go up the High Street and not meet a car. I used to take the horse and cart up there to get hay and straw when Dad wasn't well once. I was in my teens about sixteen or seventeen. I wouldn't dare now, mind you.

Kathleen Jackson

Mr Fletcher, who was blind, and Mrs Fletcher, with Mr Phipps' horse outside their shop in Albert Street, early 1950s.

The new post office, built in 1913.

Hot Rolls

Hutchinson, the baker, had a horse-drawn bread van and the delivery man would come to the door with a basketful of loaves and rolls to choose from. As often as not I was sent early in the morning to the bakehouse, to buy half a dozen rolls, steaming hot from the oven. When they were sliced for breakfast, the butter spread rapidly, melting into the roll. Hutchinson also sold vanilla slices. These were an afternoon treat as they were made at his High Street shop and confectionery bakehouse – absolutely delicious.

Roy Findley

The Talking Parrot

My grannie used to have a talking parrot and she used to hang it, often, outside the door. There was a man, a baker, lived down the bottom of the road here and his horse used to graze around the big pond. The old parrot shouted to it one day, 'Get up, go on!' like they always used to shout to the horse, and the horse moved on and the bread van went in the pond. There were all the loaves floating about in the pond.

Roy Gates

Wireless Accumulators

On the corner of Trinity Road was Mr McClymont, who was a wireless repairer. There were no radios and all that sort of thing, they were

Advertisement for Hutchinson's, bakers, 1928.

all called wirelesses and were run by a twelve volt battery and an accumulator. They used to charge the accumulators and do all the repairs there. And on the front of that building was where the garage [Stevenage Motor Company] had their first petrol pumps.

E. Woods

The Old Cottages

The cottages next door to the garage were lived in at the time by a Miss Mardlin and a Mrs Stanley. Miss Mardlin lived in the first one next to Mrs Game and Mrs Stanley was housekeeper to Mr Game's father who lived down the London Road. I drew these pictures in 1973. The back was

Cottages at 136 and 138, High Street, opposite Holy Trinity church, drawn by Mr John Walker in 1973, shortly before they were demolished.

Walter Marchant at Venables Yard, Walkern Road, early 1920s.

very old on that one cottage but the front had been put up about the same time as the church, because I can remember the pattern of the tiles was the same as the pattern of the tiles on Holy Trinity church. I've got a feeling when they were done, they said, 'Oh, we've got a few tiles over.' But the back was very old because the stairs were just blocks of wood. They were demolished because they were unsafe.

John Walker

Keeping the Fair Alive

All through the years, in the field there by the woodyard, was Mrs Smith. Now she was a Fair lady and she used to have her caravan in one of the fields there. Mr Gates used to let her have this field, her children were brought up in that field and she used to make rock for us and we used to go up there and get a penny stick of rock from her. When the war was on, they said if we didn't have a stall in the High Street, the Fair wouldn't be allowed to come back into the High Street. So she put a rock stall and a coconut stall, every 22nd September, into the High Street so that we were still allowed to keep Stevenage Fair.

Elsie Hills

Venables Yard

We lived in Walkern Road at the time. We were living in a bit of a hovel I'm afraid, and I should think this is about the only photograph ever left of Venables Yard. We lived at number one when we came to Venables Yard. Mind you, that house was only two up and one down, and I think the back of them were wooden, wooden planks or slats, whatever. I'd say they were more built in the 1700's than later. Major Venables was the man who owned those places, and he lived in the end house. I think he was a wheelwright by trade. I should have been a Hitchin man but my father was killed when I was three months old, so my mother and I lived with my grandparents, who lived in one of those houses, right until they passed on. Venables Terrace was built on Venables Yard in 1926 and we were the first council tenants in the town to have electricity.

Walter Marchant

Brushes for Everything

When I left school I was asked to stay on, but my mother was unable to cope. I had an elder brother and a younger sister who was still at school and our mother became ill so I went to work in Miss Larkinson's shop for 5/- a week. The little shop is still there but they've altered it inside. It's opposite Barclay's Bank. It's a café now, the front is, but the windows are still the same. Miss Larkinson sold toys, dolls, coco-matting, brushes and brooms. The brushes were hung in little bundles from the ceiling. There were brushes for the house, for the stove and for soft and hardware and when

Advertisement for Larkinson's shop, 1928.

someone came in to buy a brush we had to get steps and go up and untie one and sell it. She sold china tea-services, basins and jugs for the bedroom, and, of course, chamber pots.

Lily Glazebrook

Stevenage 55

The International Stores' telephone number was Stevenage 55. My mother-in-law used to ring up for her groceries. I can always remember, 'Stevenage 55.' She used to say and put on her telephone voice ... and the stuff used to come up. Everything was delivered. A man would come up and take your order, then he would deliver it. There was no class distinction, everybody had it delivered.

Arthur Richards

Weekend Delivery

In the 1930s we bought our groceries from Scarborough's, a general stores in Fishers Green Road. Mr Rogers used to come to our house and take our order which then arrived for the weekend.

Roy Findley

The Grocery Van

Jones the grocer, which is Unwin's now, he had a brother named Percy Jones who had a grocery round in Welwyn Garden City before they had any shops there. We supplied him with a 20 cwt Morris van and we sold it him for £30 and he paid us £1 a week.

John Walker

C.F. Allen's butcher's shop, High Street, 1909.

76

Voice Like a Foghorn

Of course, the biggest thing, if one really thought about it was the advent of electricity to the town in 1923 or '24. We've just [1997] gone through the business of Cabletel and all their trenches; well it was far worse when the North Metropolitan Electrical Light and Power Company came to Stevenage. It did away with the gas lamps that used to be in Walkern Road, and most of the houses that had gas installation – and you finished up with the electrical. There was an ex-Guardsman, a Sergeant in the Grenadier Guards, by the name of Robert Slocombe and he had got a voice like a foghorn. His main job was controlling a gang of people that pulled these heavy cables and laid them in the trenches, and you could hear him two streets away shouting, 'Up! Up!'

Walter Marchant

The Comic Lady

When I was a kid, there was Lewin Waby's shop. When we were good Mum used to buy us some toys. If not, well, we used to have to go on by. And also, near Palmer's Cycle Shop was an old lady that kept papers – Mrs Matthews. Her shop was just out of this world, really, it was so dark in there. She was a bit weird, this lady, she had masses of hair and wore long skirts and she just had thousands and thousands of comics, any comic that you wanted, any newspaper, and it was so dirty, but it lent to the atmosphere. She was such a

ELECTRIC COOKING IS CHEAP

ON THE NORTHMET CONTRACT RATE

ASK FOR AN INVITATION TO THE NEXT DEMONSTRATION AT YOUR NORTHMET SHOWROOM:

38, HIGH STREET, STEVENAGE.
Telephone: STEVENAGE 215.

Advertisement for Northmet, 1928.

character, I used to love to get in there and of course you always tried to get out without paying. She used to let you sort everything out.

Louise Richards

We Had To Be Patient

When people came to buy coco-matting they would perhaps have a yard and a half, and we had to take some binding and, with a thread and needle, bind it at the side. Oh it was hard work and made our fingers sore. And then, of course, we sold wall-paper and that was kept upstairs on shelves, and the people who wanted wall-paper would come up there and we used to have to take out a roll and stretch it out and the lady would say, 'Oh yes, I think I like that,' and then, 'What's that one?' and we had to be very patient with them.

Lily Glazebrook

The Hedge is Still There

When I first started work, my brothers moved up here and the Lawrence Avenue house wasn't big enough. We heard that Mr Game had a house called Gable Cottage, at 27 London Road, and we rented that from him. In front of where it was is the Land Registry Office now. As you come out of Tesco's main entrance, going towards the Open Market, there's a hedge there that I planted in 1936. Mr Game he used to go to Yarmouth, I think, every year, with Mr Lines and Mr Stutley and when he came back he said, 'John, I've ordered

some shrubs and when they come I want you to put them in the front.' so I had to dig the hedge up and put them in and that's still there.

John Walker

Get Everything in Albert Street

One of the shops in Albert Street was Fraser's, a haberdashery shop that sold everything like cottons and material. And there was Blackwell's, the chemist, then, further down there was Fletcher's, with all the paraffin and then there was Chittenden's, who had furniture. When I was a child, Alf Thody the butcher was at the top of Albert Street. We used to go in there and get faggots on a Friday night. Of course, they used to do all the slaughtering there as well. You could get everything in Albert Street. People did almost as much shopping there as they

London Road, *c.* 1910.

Alf Wootten (left) and Wilby Nye working in the rockery at Six Hills Nursery.

did in the High Street. I used to work in the butcher's shop near Smeaton's in Albert Street, with Lena and Ken Armison. I must have been there for about twenty years.

Louise Richards

Pigs Squealing

We had Thody's the butchers opposite and it was rather awful for children living there. On Tuesdays, when the pigs came from market, they used to slaughter them there and you would hear the pigs squealing and then it would all be washed down. Of course it wouldn't be on today, it wouldn't be allowed for hygiene reasons, but it was all pretty grim.

Dorothy Storton

Six Hills

There were so many footpaths to Bedwell, and to Ivory's farm that used to be down there, with all his chickens and turkeys. Then there used to be a nursery with all flowers, beautiful flowers, Elliott's Nursery at Six Hills. My two brothers worked there and there were foot paths all the way round the Six Hills. Those hills seem as though they have got smaller to me, they were so big in our day.

Elsie Hills

They Were Characters

There was a fish shop, Leggett's, run by the two Leggett ladies. They always wore black skirts and grey or white blouses, then they had their

First Stevenage Scout Troop, 1940, photographed in a field belonging to the Barclay family, adjacent to the Scout headquarters in Baldock Road. Mr Roach is fourth from the left in the back row.

hair sort of parted in the middle, done round with rings round the ears, like earphones. They were characters too. They always had their fish displayed outside, all lovely and fresh.

Louise Richards

Boat up the High Street

There was a flood in the High Street once. There was a sudden downpour and it flooded. Coof Field, the fireman, he went up, and he and a chap, who worked at Shelford and Crowe, by the name of King, I think, got a boat out and rowed up the High Street. That was well pre-war.

John Walker

Quality Stuff

At one time there was a ladies' dress shop, Elsie Smith, next to Lines' the ironmongers. They always had quality stuff, quite expensive. If you went in there and bought anything and it didn't suit, she didn't like you to take it back.

Louise Richards

Sixpenny Tea

Morning and evening we always used to go over and get a jug of tea from Steer's, for sixpence. Two or three of us used to put our pennies in to make up the sixpence. Mr MacKinnon used to keep the Marquis of Lorne and he used to stand outside and Mr Steers

A display in the window of
the Co-operative Store, High
Street, *c.* 1960.

Goldfinch shoe shop (later Hawkes) on the corner of High Street and Orchard Road, 1920s.

used to stand outside and exchange a few words at one another.

John Walker

Out of Town Shopping

We've always shopped in the High Street. I still do if I can, but of course, you can't get things now, you've got to go to the town centre. We didn't go to the town centre for a long, long time. If we wanted anything big we used to go to Welwyn Garden City, to the Stores, or occasionally to Hitchin, to the market. In those days, if we wanted anything particular, of course we went to London, because it's not very far. I used to go up with my father because he was a schoolteacher up there for forty years and I often used to go up on the train with him in the morning. He went on the 7 o'clock train, well, it was cheaper, it was the 'workman's.' I'd say, 'I'll come up with you, then Dad,' and I used to go up with him. He went to school and then I would wander around London – I daren't do that now.

Louise Richards

CHAPTER 7

War

Mrs Smith's stall in the High Street
kept the fair alive during the Second
World War. The white building in the
background, protected with sandbags,
became the mother and baby clinic and
the school dentist's surgery, with the
nurse's flat above.

Cowshed Factory

I got bombed out in London and I saw the advert for instrument making engineering in Stevenage and applied for it. This was in 1940, when I was just about seventeen. I came to Stevenage and the first place I went was the Labour Exchange to see Mr Archer and, lo and behold, the chappie who was standing behind me was by the name of Mr Peacock and I was introduced to him and we went down in his car to Bedwell Lane. There we went into what we called 'The Cowshed,' just a brick building and the first thing the governor said, 'Can you work one of these?' which was a south bend. I had never worked on a south bend but I had been on a Bowley. 'OK,' he said, 'The job's yours. Start Monday.' From there I found some rooms in the Old Town, then I started work. There were three lads there, three of us all came from London. The governor, he also came from Chingford and the other governor, he came from Brookman's Park – W.H. Saunders and Albert Peacock.

Arthur Cotts

No Time for Stress

I was called up in 1940 and I was in the Hertfordshire and Bedfordshire Regiment and after initial training we moved down to Cornwall, where we did coastal duties, patrols. I was single and it was a great thing, being in the army and my mate and I volunteered to go abroad. I was posted to the Intelligence Officer as a driver and batman and we went all the way from Alamein right up to Tunis, right through all the desert and had plenty of dodging and ducking to do. Anyway, when that finished we landed at Salerno in Italy, and then came back for the invasion of Europe. And we had a good hiding round near Caen. I had my own sergeant killed next to me and we also lost our adjutant, the orderly room clerk and no end of infantry. So we had a good hiding there. After we had the sergeant killed next to me, we buried him in twenty minutes, then just moved on again. No time to have stress or trauma in those days, you just carried on.

John Walker

Well, Damn Hitler

I was married at Hitchin Registry Office on 3rd September 1938. We wanted children very much but decided to wait a year. At the end of that year it was, of course, 3rd September 1939 and war had been declared. We spent all night talking about whether we should think of having a child at that time. Bill suddenly said, 'Well damn Hitler, if you don't have children there's no point in having wars, you might just as well give up!' We had a son in June 1940.

Eileen Harding

Look-out Tree

We joined the National Defence before the Home Guard and we were issued with ammunition to be used to start with. We had a big look-out tower in a tree at Chells Green. We had a ladder and we used to go up and get in there and look out. I was in number seven platoon. The officer was Mr Bowie, Jock Bowie, that used to work at the ESA. Our headquarters were at the Motor Company.

Stanley Marriott

Twelve-hour Shift

After a few months at the ESA I was transferred to putting the ammunition boxes together. I can't remember how long I continued doing that but then, because the run on the ammunition boxes was getting more urgent, they decided to run what they called a twelve hour shift in the woodworking machine shop. Because I was single I had to transfer to doing night work and we did seven in the morning to seven at night with about three hours' break for two weeks, but in between we had two days off and then we transferred to night work which was seven o'clock at night to seven o'clock in the morning and there again we had two nights off. Sometimes during those times when we were on nights we used to catch a workman's train in the morning and go and spend the day in London and then come back to work at night. It was about one and threepence in old money, return, then.

Enid Bates

First Class Conditions

We had a very primitive, slow burning combustion stove for our heating, no water laid on, only outside where the trough was. In the winter it got frozen. When the winter did come, one of the chaps had to go round to his digs in the London Road and walk back with a kettle, so we could get water and if it snowed we used to have to boil the snow down on the slow burner. Those were our first class conditions. Our main work, ninety per cent of it, was on brass, like bases for shell cases and also for compass cases. We were going quite well really, until Mr Wild came from the HRD and we went with his help, leaps and bounds, no doubt about it. We had so much work going on there, that there was another barn at the side which was full of cars, where people in Stevenage had laid their cars up, so we had to have them out and we had that part too.

Arthur Cotts

You Went Everywhere by Bike

I cycled backwards and forwards to Letchworth. You went everywhere by bike. I don't know what we'd have done without our bikes. You had to go to the Labour Exchange and sign when you were twenty. I was working at the time at Letchworth, so I had to go to the Labour Exchange there. Then my father knew the governor at Saunders and he had a word with him about it and I got a job there. My choice was the Land Army, but there were no vacancies. Saunders was in Bedwell Lane. Well it is pulled down now, of course, it was part of the town centre, I think Westgate goes through now, where it was. That's where I met my husband.

Mrs I. Cotts

A Christmas party for W.H. Saunders' staff, held in the ESA canteen, 1940s.

No Time For Breakfast

I used to get up about half-past six and my mum would say, 'Come on, and have this breakfast,' and I used to say, 'I can't have the breakfast, give me a piece of toast,' and I'd run up the High Street to catch the train Of course the station was way up the end of the High Street and the train came in at half-past seven to take us to Letchworth. We started work at eight, and it was eight until eight, we had to work, Saturdays until four and Sundays until one. And because our train at night left at quarter to eight, and that was the last one, they said that we had to leave at half past seven. We'd come out of work at half past seven, over the Spirella Bridge, because we were at the Spirella then, because Irvings took Spirella over, and we'd wait for the train to come into the station. Sometimes it would be late, sometimes it would be early, but most of all it would be late. We'd get to Hitchin siding and the siren would go and we'd sit and sit and sit, some nights until ten o'clock, before they'd let us go. So our life was nil, practically. But what part we did have of it, we enjoyed.

Elsie Hills

Full Up With Soldiers

I was fourteen when the war began and I had just started work at the Spirella factory. I was living in Stevenage, in Whitesmead Road and I used to go on the train at 7.15 every morning. There were no buses, you had to walk from Whitesmead Road. We used sometimes to work overtime and we arrived home at 10. There was quite a crowd of us. Really, the war was terrible but we all had a good time. There was plenty went on in Stevenage I think. If you went to the Publix cinema you were lucky if there were six girls there, it'd be full up with soldiers. There were dances every night at the Town Hall and then in Pound Avenue they built that Lytton Club and there was one there Wednesdays and Sundays. As I say, we didn't realise there was a war on, it was sad really.

Thelma Bartholomew

Extra Help

As things began to develop, we used to have land girls and also after the war started we had German and Italian prisoners on the farm. They seemed to adapt very quickly. The Germans were better than the Italians. Once you showed them how to handle horses or tractors they got it very quickly. They were billeted on the old London Road. They used to fetch them with a lorry each morning. There would be a guard come with them. It was just the same when we had threshing engines, we used to have extra labour, either Italian prisoners or Land Girls. It was the same with potato picking or big jobs, you always had extra help.

Stanley Marriott

They Were Good Days

Of course, during the war it was all coupons. You couldn't buy anything without coupons. I was still working at Irving's Parachutes and I wasn't married then and I saw Mrs Hicks one day and I said to her, 'How are you managing with all your children?' 'Well, it's a bit of a job,' she said, 'but my husband's started making some little flowers out of different things and we're going to see if we can start selling them.' I said, 'Well, you make some and I'll take them to work and I'll sell them for you.' And he made me loads and I got rid of them all, for him, at work, so I said to her, 'Now with all those coupons you're getting for your children, can you afford to use them all?' so she said, 'No, I don't use them, I can't afford to keep buying clothes.' So I said, 'Well, what if I gave you some of my clothes that I don't want and you give me some coupons?' 'Ooh, lovely,' she said, so all my clothes that I didn't want I gave to her and she gave me some coupons so I could go and buy new clothes. They were good days. Everybody helped each other.

Elsie Hills

A Bit Difficult

Clothes rations were a bit difficult really, but I think aunts used to give me a couple of coupons. You know, you sort of shared round and I remember Mr Hawkes at the shoe shop, when I got married I wanted a pair of silver shoes and instead of seven coupons he let me have them for three. I worked on parachutes in the war. I made, oh, tons of underclothes with parachute silk, because we started working with pure silk, but then that got sabotaged so they started on nylon. It was quite interesting

Practice with a stirrup pump, Second World War.

A Second World War ARP parade through the High Street.

really. That was the only job I had. Once you got into work you couldn't leave.

Thelma Bartholomew

Queen Mary Lorries

You'd get a lot of RAF with their Queen Mary lorries with crashed aeroplanes parked there, as they were passing through. Queen Mary lorries were the prime movers. They had these very long trailers, low-loaders, which were about, I think, 52 or 60 feet long, which could take a whole fuselage of a Spitfire or a Messerschmitt or whatever they were taking back to their camp. They were very, very big. In those days you'd get

one where the bus stop is now in the middle of the town there, opposite the White Lion. They would park there and all us kids would be scrambling all over them. I was only about seven at the time, seven or eight. We didn't need adventure playgrounds in those days.

Wilf Neilson

The Night Shift

We had so many operators and we wanted to use them, so Wild suggested that we run a night shift. We could start at eight o'clock in the evening, but a lot of the people started at ten o'clock because some of them lived out in the outlying villages – like

Walkern, Woolmer Green, Knebworth — and from Hitchin. So the main time was from ten o'clock until eight o'clock next morning, but they could start beforehand. Some of the part-timers we had on nights came from the Warren in the London Road, which were chappies like the wounded, or in bad health, on light duties and things like that, and we used to have somewhere round about ten of them on night shift. They didn't do sweeping up jobs, but they all worked various machines and power tools. The women who worked there were all about the same age – eighteen or nineteen years old. They came from Walkern and places like that.

Arthur Cotts

Rockets and Doodle-bugs

The place was blacked out and when the siren went at night, somebody used to go out to watch, so that if anything should happen, he would come in and tell us and we would prepare. As a matter of fact, one morning we went out early, after the siren went, and we actually saw the rockets being launched off the coast of Holland. You saw a spark and then you actually saw the rockets and the vapour, and it gave it out on the radio that early morning workers had seen the rockets being launched. There wasn't a shelter. When we heard what we called the 'doodle bugs' go over we used to run out and watch them and pray that they wouldn't stop.

Mrs I. Cotts

Air-raid Shelter

The only air-raid shelter was just up Back Lane, next to Southend Farm. It was brick built and had double doors at each end. It was quite a large one. There were seats in there. No one ever did use it.

Roy Gates

Blackout

The Publix Cinema had a blackout over the door and you went into the first bit, then there was another curtain and you were into the cinema. I remember once in the Astonia cinema having to lie on the floor because a doodle-bug was going over. I used to enjoy horrific films – *The Mummy*, *The Old Dark House* and films with Boris Karloff.

Betty Game

Civil Defence

The Civil Defence was very well organised, yes, very. I think somehow in our lot they were trained better than soldiers that went straight out. I mean I could do most of the things now. Jock Bowie, he was Scots, but he was very good.

Stanley Marriott

The Home Guard

During the war the Home Guard was on the corner of Trinity Road and I was in it. We were one of the largest Home Guard units in the country, I think. There were over 1,000 people in C Company. Major Howard was in charge of us. Dicky White, he had a Military Cross, they were both in the 1914 war. Stan Stutley was officer of the section I was in. I was in intelligence section – don't shout it!

Roy Gates

Gas Masks

And everybody carried a gas mask. I remember when war broke out we were at the farm. There was an air-raid warning and a plane came down on Camp's Hill and all this black smoke poured out. We had these gas masks and we put them on because we thought there was gas.

Stanley Marriott

Spitfires and Parachutes

At one time we needed to make quite a lot of castors for the Spitfire, for the tail wheel and they were quite red-hot jobs. They were produced by the hundred at the finish. They were delivered to Castle Bromwich. Then we used to do an inertia-weight, which used to release the parachute and all that type of equipment.

Arthur Cotts

Cost of Living

My fare was no more than two shillings in old money and I know we used to go to the pictures for sixpence and have a bar of chocolate for twopence and a box of face powder for threepence at Woolworth's because nothing was any more than sixpence in those days at Woolworth's. We had a coal ration. I can't remember how much but then my father worked at the ESA and of course he used to get bits of wood so that was all right.

Thelma Bartholomew

The British Restaurant

At times when my parents were both out we would go to the British Restaurant. This was during the war, when you would go up to the Town Hall and sit on benches with all the other workers, that's where you got good basic meals. There was rationing on at the time. And of course, with the A1 going through the middle of the town, where the National Westminster Bank is at the moment, was the WVS – the forces' canteen. My mother and my mother's sister-in-law worked there during the war in the evenings, all voluntary. They used to come back and tell us the stories of who was going through there, like the time they had a two-part convoy come in once a fortnight, of 6,000 Canadians who virtually wrecked the place and it had to be closed for repair. I think most of those then finished up in Dieppe, captured on a commando raid.

Wilf Neilson

Arthur and Louise Richards, outside the Dun Cow, Letchmore Road, on their wedding day in 1942.

Shoved Out

We married in 1942 and then of course I had to go in the forces until 1946. For the first ten years of our married life we lived with Louie's mum and dad in Letchmore Road – the houses are not there now – opposite the Dun Cow, and our wedding reception was at the Dun Cow. We were married at St Nicholas'. They were marrying them, on that particular day, starting at 8 o'clock in the morning and the thing was, we had to go into the vestry to sign the registers and when we came out, we looked and there wasn't not one single soul of our family there. Our lot had been shoved out and the next lot were in, ready. So we walked down the aisle all on our own.

Arthur Richards

I Saw the German's Face

We used to have tons of planes over. The nearest I've been to a German plane was near Roy Shelford's bungalow and I was in the opposite field with a tractor. It was foggy, very foggy, this Dornier Bomber came so low because it was coming in to shoot up the train at Langley siding. I could see the German's face plain as I'm looking at you and he just skimmed the tree there and went straight down and shot up the train. I can remember the chap's face.

Stanley Marriott

When the Americans Came

Being in a very rural area, I can always remember father bringing home eggs when he'd been working on farms, and you'd get plenty of natural stuff. Of course, gardens and allotments were always very high on the list so there were always vegetables. Everybody, as I remember it, was very fit in those days. No one was over-weight, we were all lean. As a kid it seemed a great time, to hear these stories, they didn't really involve you. Of course, it got even more exciting after 1941 when the Americans came into the war, because you used to get their lorries powering through the High Street with a black outrider in front of them. They used to go through very fast. Some used to stop and everyone was asking, 'Got any gum, chum?' There were a lot of them. They were very friendly, we found, and they were more affluent than our troops.

Wilf Neilson

Evacuees

We had two evacuees with us. They came from Seven Sisters Road in London. I always remember Mrs Horsfield bringing them round. We had to have them, they just brought them on the doorstep then. Their names were Violet and Rose Scrobie, one was five and the other was seven I think, but they were nice little kids. It was awful at first. They'd got a big family and they said, 'We don't have chairs, we only have boxes to sit on.' They came down for quite a while really and then all at once they went back.

Kathleen Jackson

Search Lights

Of course we had search lights, you see. There was one on the corner of Stevenage Lodge Road on the Walkern Road. They got one in the beam one night. I was in bed and all of a sudden a bomb went down. It just missed the cowshed and came down where the cows grazed and of course it lit the farm up just like daylight and the stacks that had just been thatched,

so they were all shining white and they looked like a lot of houses. Then I remember getting out of bed pretty quickly and going to get a pail and some grit to put the fire out but it lit up all that area and the plane was still circling above.

Stanley Marriott

They Looked After Themselves

I used to cart the prisoners of war about during the war. I used to take a lorry load of them, pick them up from their camps. They were all over the place, there was one just the other side of

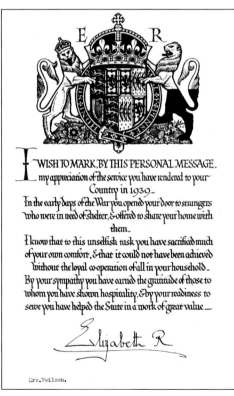

I WISH TO MARK BY THIS PERSONAL MESSAGE my appreciation of the service you have rendered to your Country in 1939. In the early days of the War you opened your door to strangers who were in need of shelter, & offered to share your home with them. I know that to this unselfish task you have sacrificed much of your own comfort, & that it could not have been achieved without the loyal co-operation of all in your household. By your sympathy you have earned the gratitude of those to whom you have shown hospitality, & by your readiness to serve you have helped the State in a work of great value

Elizabeth R

Mrs. Neilson.

Mrs Neilson's copy of the message of thanks from the Queen to those who took in evacuees during the Second World War.

93

Ware at Widford, one at Royston on the heath there, one at Trumpington, Cambridge. There were other little ones. There was a little one, an Italian one, at Redhill, a little hamlet near The Moon and Stars at Cumberlow Green way. They weren't mixed in the camps. The little one at Redhill was Italian but all the other camps were German. Mostly I used to take them to the farms, they did hedging and ditching and all that work. To start with they had an armed guard with them, and then after that they didn't, they just had a chief man and they used to look after themselves. They took their food and that, their dixies and stuff with them, and lit a fire and heated the dixies. Yes, they used to sort of fend for themselves.

Roy Gates

Italian Workers

The prisoners of war were quite friendly. We were kind to them. The Italians used to dig the ditches right through to Monkswood. There'd be an armed guard there with a rifle and there'd be about twenty prisoners cutting the hedges down and doing various jobs. The land girls were very, very good. The funny thing about it was, if we had land girls, say, that had been in a beauty parlour or something over at St Albans, they'd adapt better than the local girls once they were shown how to handle a tractor. They used to cut corn with a tractor and they were very good with animals too, bringing up calves.

Stanley Marriott

German Toymakers

Some of them worked in the woodyard. I don't know how they got there. I think they were Italians. They used to make toys. The Germans used to make a lot of toys, jumping men and things you pull on a stick and that sort of thing. And basket work, the Italians used to make basketwork. They used to make lighters and things. They used to sit and bash things out of an old kettle. They'd make lighters and all sorts of instruments. They were clever.

Roy Gates

Wartime Romance

I went as far as the Maas in Holland and then we had so many casualties there that we were posted back to Northern Ireland and I was drafted to the Royal Scots, the Eighth Battalion, and moved to a place in Belgium. I was billeted in this house, only for three weeks, for a rest period and I saw this lady, in there, the daughter of the house, once or twice. I think she must have been mostly working in the field. Anyway, I was just about to move off, got my kit ready to move off, and she came out with tears in her eyes. She wanted to marry me. Well, I'd made no advances to her – they were very strict out there, being a Catholic country, very, very strict indeed. I said, 'Well, I don't know what's going to happen, crossing the Rhine and all that.' Anyhow, I thought about it, I didn't commit myself, but any rate, we crossed the Rhine and the Elbe and I thought about her and started corresponding and we decided to get married. I had to

Albert Street's party in the Parish Room (tin hut), Basil's Road, celebrating the end of the Second World War.

Albert Street celebrates the end of the Second World War.

Albert Street celebrates the end of the war.

have written consent from my mother. They were very strict, you see. I was thirty. My birth certificate had to go to the Burghermaster to say that everybody agreed to the marriage – my side and her side. It makes a happy marriage if everybody agrees to it and then we got married in January 1946, in the church at Haarlem in Belgium. When we came back we lived in London Road with my mother. Before we left Belgium, one of my wife's friends always used to say to me, 'Johnny, you have six children.' We went home, and didn't have any the first year. The next year we had one child and when we went over to see her again, she said, 'Johnny, you have six children,' and so it went on and on. After six years we never went to see her any more! We've got four sons and two daughters.

John Walker

The Siren

We had a bomb over Fairview Road way, but that was all. The siren used to go but nothing really happened. I can't remember any shelters, not in Stevenage – there were at Letchworth. If there was another war now it would be different, you'd dread it now, but then you were young and all you thought about was going out and having a good time.

Thelma Bartholomew

CHAPTER 8

New Town

The Town Centre Team: architects, quantity surveyors, clerk of works, contractors' personnel. Ray Gorbing is fifth from the left.

More Money in My Pocket

It was actually during the war, 1944, I first read about the New Town. To me obviously as a newspaper reporter that was very exciting because it meant more readers and more sales of papers and hopefully therefore more money in my pocket so I looked forward to it very much.

Don Hills

Cut Off

When the New Town came it cut the Old Town people completely off from their way of life, because we were quite a large kind of village. Of course, it would happen because progress came, didn't it, with the new ways of cooking and manufacturing, but many of the old town people did lose that country way of life when the New Town came and we often used to wish that we had been left as a village and the New Town had grown up separately.

Lily Glazebrook

Tremendous Changes

I understand what you're saying extremely well. I'm very grateful that, as a boy, in Essex I saw the last of the old farming practices. I think life in Stevenage would have changed without the Development Corporation, but because of the scale of development of the New Town, taking a population of 6,000, to a projected population of 60,000 – that was a tremendous change. But, irrespective of the 1946 New Towns Act and what that brought, there were plans for the expansion of Stevenage prior to the war.

Alan Cudmore

Silkin's Visit

Well it was a great, charged atmosphere. There was a queue stretching from the old Town Hall, down Orchard Road and round the corner almost to the Northmet Showroom in the High Street, well before that meeting started, and not everyone could get into the hall. Orchard Road itself was packed with people who couldn't get in and there were loudspeakers to relay the proceedings inside to those on the outside. Silkin was driven to the Town Hall in a black limousine and he was then accompanied into the hall and on to the stage where he got some boos, of course, the moment he took his place on the stand. There were one or two moments when Silkin seemed to lose his cool and he virtually told them, 'Well, whether you like it or not, it's going to happen.' Silkin had toured the town in the afternoon and he was followed wherever he went, of course, by press people and newsreel cameras. I remember one particular moment when he was in Fairview Road and Mr Vincent was leaning on his garden gate and Silkin stopped to speak to him and of course he complained to Silkin that, under the plan as it had been published, Fairview Road was to disappear and therefore he was going to lose his house and he wasn't very happy about that.

Silkin said, 'We can build you another house,' and I remember Vincent turning and pointing to a lovely tree in his garden. He said, 'Yes, you may be able to build me another house, but can you build me another tree like that?' which got some pretty good headlines in the national papers, you can imagine.

Don Hills

The Challenge

I found Town Planning interesting because as an architect you were designing in a small world – a house or a factory – but as a town planner you were working in a much wider field, you were meeting people, you were meeting so many other disciplines. It is a dual role as an architect and as a town planner. This sort of thing hadn't been done before, it was really a challenge, not only for me but also for the people who organised it.

Ray Gorbing

Worried to Death

Mr Browning farmed at Half Hyde – that was a big farm, about five hundred acres – and when the New Town came he was worried to death you know, because he was getting on in years and he had been there so long and that's what killed him the worry of losing the farm.

Stanley Marriott

Cyril Richardson, seated left, on the fence, is seen selling the last herd of attested pedigree Ayrshire cattle for R.V. Marriott, at Fairlands Farm, Friday 11 October 1957.

Ray Gorbing presented to the Queen on her visit to the New Town Centre.

We're Not Having This

The Town Centre took a hell of a long time. I was put in charge of designing the first stages, that's Queensway, Queen's Square, and all the rest of it. It was decided that we would do it on the pedestrian principle. There hadn't been a pedestrian town centre in England up to that time. To get the information on it, I went to Rotterdam, where there was a quite a small pedestrian centre. We got the designs done and took them to the Ministry and they said, 'Oh no, no, we're not having this,' and I had to de-design Queensway with a road through it. But we were so sure that a pedestrian centre was the right thing to do that we lobbied the Ministry and it took two years to get their agreement.

Ray Gorbing

First Phase Shops

The first appointment I had with the Development Corporation was in the letting of the first phase shops in the Town Centre. The first phase was nearing completion and the anchor tenants had already been decided upon and their premises worked out on plan – such as Boots, Woolworth's, Sainsbury's, Fine Fare and the Co-op. They were the cornerstones of the development. The other units were of varying sizes – what we call standard units – and they were to be granted as leases for twenty-one years.

Alan Cudmore

The Big New Co-op

When the shopping centre of the New Town was going to be built, I remember it was Whitsun, and my middle son was about eight months old and we all went along the London Road to where there was this big hoarding up, with a list of all the shops that were going to open there. We were all so thrilled because we were going to have a Marks & Spencer's, a Woolworth's, a Co-op. We couldn't believe it and that was the start of the New Town Centre and when it was eventually built, the big Co-op, we all stood outside and looked at all the lovely mosaic work that it had outside.

Kate Cope

Your Last Season

When the Corporation served notice on my great-uncle that the land would be required for development purposes, they told him,'You'd better start getting rid of your stock' – he had quite a bit of livestock there – 'and if you are growing anything, this is your last season for growing.' Then they didn't want it quite as early as they thought they would, because of the arguments as to whether it should be a pedestrian town centre or not, which delayed things. W.H. Sanders had set

up in Bedwell Farm and I know that their lathes were in what was the former cowshed and this was a bit of a saviour to my uncle. When he got up in the morning he could still wander round and not milk the cows, but at least he could talk to the guys who were using the farm buildings. When they moved out into their new premises, I'm afraid he literally packed up and died.

Don Hills

The Lost Columns

We built the Town Centre of pre-cast concrete and we decided we would cast it in the town. We found that when we started driving the first columns into the ground, we just lost them, eighty columns. Stevenage is very unstable underneath. Right across the Town Centre there's a huge band of this stuff that was deposited during the ice-age, it's chalk and a lot of water. There were springs there and we had to stuff these springs up with concrete. Underneath the town square there's all sorts of funny things, I can tell you.

Ray Gorbing

Unique Town Centre

Stevenage Town Centre was unique, even within the New Town movement, because we were, as landlords, in direct relationship with traders. No land had been put out to property companies to develop and every tenant was a lessee of the Corporation and we could, therefore,

Building the first phase of the Town Centre, 1958.

through leases, control the actual trades and specify what they were permitted to sell. OK, it became difficult with people like Woolworth's, who tended to sell everything, and jokingly their lease was referred to as an elephant clause - but by and large it worked and it also gave you the opportunity to adjust your rents according to the profit level or turnover of the individual traders.

Alan Cudmore

Joy Ride

The statue, the little mother and child by Belski – 'Joy Ride' – that was me, I suppose. I rather liked it and I got him to do it and we put it on the top there and funnily enough – well nobody knows – but underneath that

statue there are about six different stones that I brought from various parts of the world where I'd been on holiday.

Ray Gorbing

Wonderful

I can remember coming here on the Green Line Bus from Golders Green, on the 716, and arriving in the Old Town on a snowy morning. We had to find Sish Lane and go along to this house in Sish Lane and talk about houses and we couldn't believe it, we were put into a mini-bus with two other couples and taken around to see four houses. Having lived for six and a half years without a place of our own and to be given the choice of four houses, we just could not believe it. My husband

102

and I between us decided we wanted a C17 and we didn't let anybody else hear what we were saying, because we thought there might not be enough to go around and we wanted to make sure of one. C17 houses were in the Roebuck area, and to have three bedrooms and a large living room and a kitchen of our own, and a porch, an open porch that even had a light in it, so that when people came you could put this light on and welcome them into the house – we just could not believe it, and our own garden. Wonderful!

Kate Cope

Wet Sunday Afternoon

I was born in Finchley, North London, then moved to Stevenage when I was fourteen, in 1951. I remember coming off the train one wet Sunday afternoon and walking down the High Street, which was of course absolutely deserted and looking up at a notice board for Stevenage Archery Club, which I thought must be a wild piece of excitement.

Peter Blagg

Shortage of Bricks

We designed the houses, the buildings, the shops, but we had to use the materials that were available at the time, we had to adapt the designs to the materials. Having designed the first houses at Bedwell in brick, we found that there weren't any bricks to be had. The supply from the brick-works out at Bedford had dried up, so we had to use pre-fabricated systems which weren't very good.

Ray Gorbing

Acres of Mud

I can remember Six Hills Way being just one long squelchy walk. It was terrible.

We kept on appointing extra midwives. They needed houses and the Corporation offered us one in what became Valley Way, which was just acres of mud with houses popping up. I remember one of the other midwives saying, 'You can't possibly ask a midwife to live right out there.' It was unheard of. But gradually the mud dried out and the roads came and she did quite well up there.

Stella Kestin

We Loved It

I was born 1935, in Islington and lived there until I married. My husband was a true Londoner, who said, 'No way will I ever go to one of these New Towns.' But when Michael, my eldest son, was born, we came down for a week-end to visit my husband's brother who lived in Marymead and immediately he said, 'I shall get a job and get a house here.' The main reason was, we wanted a house as we were living in two rooms, but once we got here, we loved it. We came in May 1958, to The Muntings and are still there.

Barbara Burley

John and Elizabeth Amess with Ian and Keith at home in Stevenage, 5 October 1958.

Old Town Shops

We moved on 3 April 1954 – impressed on my mind for ever. When we moved in there were four houses at the end of my road that were converted into shops and we had a chemist, a green grocer, and a newsagent. Anyway, we used to go to the Old Town because that's where all the shops were, and there weren't any buses, not in the early days, so we used to walk the two miles to the shops. There weren't any roads built then, so we used to have to walk down to the Roebuck and walk all along the old London Road, pushing the pram.

Kate Cope

We Came in the Furniture Van

My wife and I and baby son eventually moved to Stevenage, all in a removal van. It was an absolute thrill to come and move into a new house. We couldn't get over the fact that our house had two front doors, one where you went into a sort of porch entrance, and the front door next to it where you went into the coal part and through from there into the kitchen.

John Amess

Tie a Ribbon to the House

When I came, I moved in on my own as my husband was away.

I had the day off to move in, but had to go to work, at Hendon, the next day. I had a car to get to work. When I got home I couldn't find the road and drove round in a panic. I went to Police Station and said, 'I only moved in yesterday and I can't find my house'. The policeman got a car out and I followed him. He suggested I tie ribbon to the house.

Sylvia Molloy

We Arrived in 1958

I was born 1923, in Brixton and we later moved to Burnt Oak. In the war I married a sailor and we had two rooms in Mum and Dad's house. We went on the list for a house, but there was not a chance. When Stevenage New Town was built, our council wrote and asked if we would be prepared to move. My husband had to get a job here. He came as a catering manager to a factory in the New Town. We arrived in 1958, in Valley Way to a house built as infill where previously there had been a field. My husband died after six years and I've been on my own since, still renting the same house. My brother-in-law came later and worked at Kodak.

Patricia Palmer

How Grateful We Were

Other than using the shops I don't think we had a lot to do with the people in the Old Town. I think it was later that I began to get to know people in the Old Town. We didn't find any hostility towards us, it was more of a gentle leg-pull than anything really serious. I think I always used to explain to the people in the Old Town just how grateful we were to move out of bomb-ravaged London into a new town with a new house. I realised what they had given up.

John Amess

Made Them Welcome

There weren't any churches in the new areas at first. I was involved in Sunday School teaching at Holy Trinity and we decided that we would take the Sunday Schools to the people. I think that was the Revd Ted Harper's brainchild really, because he was all for the New Town. A family in Broadview allowed us to use their room for a Sunday School class, so children used to come from that area, all from the New Town, quite a number, on Sunday afternoons. We did this for about six months. I think some of the New Town people thought that we didn't want them to come, so we tried to make them welcome. There was quite a lot in the press about opposition – after all, that makes news. Later there was talk about 'New Town Blues.' Some of the people who came weren't very happy to start with because there were no shops and no entertainment and it was too quiet for them. A lot of people used to go back to London at weekends. The trains were full of New Town people going home on Saturdays, from the old station at the top of Julians Road.

Betty Game

Holy Trinity Sunday schoolchildren, 1960s.

I Felt Sorry For Them

I certainly wasn't aware of any hostility. I'd read about it, but I didn't come across it personally, but I think perhaps it was your attitude to the people you were with. If your attitude was that you were prepared just to mix in, it didn't make any difference. I didn't find it hostile. I felt sorry for them. I felt sorry for the people, some of whom had lost out because of it. I know they got compensation but it's still not the same, is it?

Kate Cope

I Like It Here

I thought we'd come to Stevenage for two years. I thought, 'Well, two years will be enough experience of this sort of thing and then go on and get another job somewhere. 'But it was the challenge, I think, that kept us here and quite honestly, I liked Stevenage, I liked the people that came out and I liked everything about the town. I liked being here and we've stayed here ever since, fifty years now, and you get involved. I got involved in Stevenage Tennis Club, when it was behind the White Lion, in 1952, and I've been chairman ever since.

Ray Gorbing

We Knew the Country Code

My husband had been evacuated during the war to the country. He knew all the trees and birds, whereas I knew nothing. I loved it. I took the children blackberrying, near the Roebuck. Fairlands Valley was cornfields. A man in Hertford Road had an orchard in his back garden, near Spencer's nursery, where we used to buy our rose bushes. My son used to love playing in the stubble cornfields. We used to put the children in a big pram and walk miles.

Barbara Burley

The Last Lark Sang

I think we became countrified with that bit of valley at the back. My husband and I loved watching the birds. I used to walk home across the valley, when they were beginning to make it a park. I was walking diagonally across from Six Hills Way, on a lovely sunny evening, when a lark sprang up and sang – the last one I saw over there – I can still see it now.

Patricia Palmer

Community of Pioneers

I think we were aware of the fact that we were pioneers. A group of families in that area recognized that. One or two of them eventually returned home, but the other families all became great friends and we're still friends now. We worked together, solved our problems, ploughed our way through the mud and our wives all went to the clinic

Children in a garden in Valley Way, *c.* 1959. Left to right: Catherine and Linda Roberts, Judith Palmer.

The old and the new. A painting by Roy Findley of Primrose Hill cottages with Chauncy House flats in the background, c. 1956.

together and one thing and another. So, yes, I think we were quite a community of pioneers.

John Amess

A Lot of Loneliness

The people moving into the New Town usually were so thrilled at having a house of their own, but on the other hand, a lot of them were very lonely, because they missed the corner shop, they missed their mums and grandmums round the corner. There was quite a lot of loneliness. They were thrilled with the openness of Stevenage, the greenness, and some of them had quite a long walk to come down to the clinic because there was no other way of getting from parts of Bedwell down to the High Street. Then, of course, there was the Bailey Bridge across the London Road, to get people to the industrial area.

Stella Kestin

Rooms to the Acre

We started off by building at a certain density, a certain number of habitable rooms per acre, then the national finances got into a bit of a pickle and we somehow had to find ways and means of building houses more cheaply. One way was to build not houses but flats, because you get more to the acre. The densities we had to work to were constantly changing.

Ray Gorbing

Children Get Together

In the early 1960s when all the new C. of E. churches had become established, we held sports days for children from the different churches, to try to make people feel that we all belonged to one another, to integrate everyone. The first one was held on Bury Mead, organised by Holy Trinity. We gave a cup for the winning church. Then several other churches took it in turns to organise it and it was held in different parts of the town. This helped us to get to know many people in the New Town and we are still friends to this day.

Betty Game

Sharon Findley in her garden at Primrose Hill cottages, now demolished, 1956.

Building Roman Catholic Churches

When we first arrived in Stevenage there was only a hut up at Bedwell. The nearest Catholic church was in the Old Town, so we used that. There was a coach that went round Stevenage picking up Catholics from the New Town to take them up to Bedwell and then later on when the Bedwell church, St Joseph's, was built, the hut was moved to Shephall. It was just an old army hut and it was there for several years until they built St Hilda's at Shephall, but that was really within walking distance.

John Amess

More Churches

St Peter's church, which I attended, wasn't up at Marymead as it is now. It was just a hut in the Hertford Road, and then eventually a church was built at Marymead and then the hut in Hertford Road was taken over by St Paul's Methodist church until they had their own permanent building at the back of the Roebuck shops.

Kate Cope

The visit of Queen Elizabeth, the Queen Mother, to Stevenage, when she laid the foundation stone of St George's church, 14 July, 1956.

We'd Never Done This Before

One of our biggest problems was that the contractors knew that we were designing contracts of about 800, 900 or 1,000 houses. Now we'd never done this before. It even got to the stage when we set up our own little group to examine each contract, so we could fight the contractors, but it was a big problem. The contractors knew that we were quite young, inexperienced if you like, and one error multiplied by 800 times is a lot of money.

Ray Gorbing

Planning Enquiry

There were some very dilapidated cottages in Baker Street which I think, if we'd had our own way we'd have probably pulled down and that went to a Planning Enquiry and I

Father Valentine with the Guild of St Stephen (altar servers' guild), Church of the Transfiguration, Basils Road, 1934/35.

110

Old cottages in Baker Street, looking towards the High Street. The wooden building on the extreme left was the Salvation Army hut.

can remember giving evidence and arguing that the costs of restoration could never be recouped through commercial lettings, but the inspector said, 'You must restore these buildings,' and that we did. We also looked actually at moving the building that was the South End Post Office and we had a very famous architect who specialised in restoration and conversion of old buildings actually to see if we could move it from that site and put it elsewhere down the High Street, but the County Council, with its experts, decided that it should stay and the main reason for that is that it's got a Crown Post Roof in its construction. I think the Development Corporation did make efforts to conserve, but – thinking of Shephall Village and the farm buildings in Shephall Village – there's hardly anything there now that is a memory of it being the centre of a farming community, apart from, perhaps, the pub and the church.

Alan Cudmore

The Valley and the Canyon

I was involved in the campaign to save the valley. We dreaded it, first of all they were going to build houses, then this road. Joan Stapleton and I were the postmen, we went around knocking on doors with petitions. It happened just after my husband died and it got me out of the house again. We had a classy committee, but I hadn't got to the point when I dare speak out. At the same time I got involved with Tessa Peters and Betty Pickersgill who started off the idea of making the adventure playground, the Canyon. It had become a sort of

111

meeting place for many kids, but there was also rubbish dumped there, making it dangerous.

Patricia Palmer

Conservation Consciousness

We have become much more conscious of conservation. I mean, I can think of mediaeval farm buildings that were knocked down in this town and you will, rightly, say 'sacrilege,' but we hadn't quite sharpened our pencils to the extent we have now in ensuring that that things are conserved. One of the things that disappoints me is what has happened to the Old Town. I feel it was sad that the general sort of road pattern of railings and things like that were implanted on the Old Town.

Alan Cudmore

Dog Walking in the Woods

We three are great friends. We first met when dog-walking in the woods. Although we live fairly near to each other, our paths had not crossed before, even though we had sons close in age. The woods are very important in our lives. The dogs got us there first, but Pat's husband used to take the children there to watch birds. We keep our eyes open and watch what's going on. When they said they were going to enlarge the car park, we said we would chain ourselves to the trees.

Patricia Palmer, Barbara Burley, Sylvia Molloy

Dog-walkers in Fairlands Valley, with Monks and Whomerley Woods in the background. From the left: 'Pepsi', Laura Brown, Patricia Palmer with 'Jimmy', 'Sophie', Barbara Burley, Christopher Brown, Sylvia Molloy with 'Jess'.

Money, Money, Money

All the time we had to go to meetings in London with the Ministry people and usually they said, 'OK, you can do that but knock a million quid off.' It was like that, money, money, money all the time.

Ray Gorbing

Cuckoo in the Nest

The other date I think that is important, is 1978, when the housing stock that the Development Corporation had built and also the neighbourhood shops and community centres were all transferred to the Stevenage Borough Council. If one looked at this from the Urban District Council's point of view, the Development Corporation was a very big cuckoo in their small nest.

Alan Cudmore

I Want My Mum

I did feel homesick, I was very young, twenty-three and came from a big family. Nobody had any money and although London wasn't far, we couldn't afford to go back very often or they to come here. I had been used to seeing my mother every day and then, when I had the babies, there was no one to help. We turned to our neighbours. I came here on a Whitsun week end when there was a bus strike on. I was allowed to come in the furniture van, because of strike. Only a few houses had been built and we were in the first. The rooms all echoed, there was no furniture and I sat and cried, 'I want my mum!' My husband said, 'There aren't any buses.'

Barbara Burley

No Regrets

I certainly have no regrets at all about moving in to Stevenage. I think it was a tremendous privilege to move away from an old Victorian house in London, where we lived with about three or four other families, crammed into a couple of rooms, to move into a new house, in a brand new town, and be a part of the development of that town, with the countryside around. We always thought that we would consider London our home and that we would want to go back to London fairly frequently. but we very soon lost that and whenever we went back we were only too glad to leave and return to Stevenage. Bear in mind that moving from South London to Stevenage in those days was almost like emigrating. You couldn't see your family that often, you didn't have a telephone as you do now. It was a long time before we had a telephone, so letter writing was important. Our parents felt as though we'd moved to Australia.

John Amess

A Cure for Bronchitis

Until we came here my husband had bronchitis every year – we used

Alan Cudmore, Chief Estates Surveyor for the Stevenage Development Corporation, 1979.

to dread the winter. But since we came here he hasn't had it once.

Sylvia Molloy

A Range of Experience

One of the great things about working for a Development Corporation particularly if you stayed long enough, you were able to get a range of experience as a surveyor which you would not be able to get anywhere else. I stayed with the Development Corporation until it wound up in 1980 and was then appointed by the Commission for New Towns as its Principal Officer.

Alan Cudmore

Your Wife Will Love It

We were living in rented accommodation in Bushey and we wanted to buy a house. I had three jobs and Terry had two, for the deposit. We started looking at Bushey, then Knebworth, but couldn't afford anything. Then the estate agent rang and said, 'I've got just the house, your wife will love it. Don't bring her in the daytime, it looks like a military barracks, but if you bring her here at night she'll love it.' And I did. We were only going to stay two years, but twenty-three years later, we're still here.

Sylvia Molloy

Final Wish

I want to be cremated and scattered in Monks Wood.

Patricia Palmer

Still the New Town?

You'll find it still called the New Town but as it's been here for what, forty years, it should really be stopped being called the New Town, I suppose.

Wilf Neilson

CHAPTER 9

Leisure

The Bunyan Baptist church outing, late 1920s. The second lady from the left, standing, is Miss Little. Mr Dean is standing near her in a cap. Mrs Howard is the fifth lady from the right, standing. Far right, standing, is Connie Turner and the lady sitting in the chair is Edie Nye. Sixth from the left, standing, is Mrs Davies.

Arms and the Man

In the early 1920s my father started a Stevenage Dramatic Society. There were no facilities in the Town Hall for big shows at all. There were no curtains for the stage, for example. I was only a child but father and my sisters' boy friends made the footlights and the curtains. My father wanted to do good plays, so they started off with this little society producing a Shaw play, *Arms and the Man*. They produced three Shaw plays and on one occasion Bernard Shaw came and sat in the back row and I remember seeing him there.

Eileen Harding

Number Six, Come Back

The Sunday schools used to run a day out in the summer. For a little money we could go to Bedford and I always remember the Bunyan Baptist church had hired the double-decker bus and we went upstairs. We went to Bedford for the day and the tea was given us at the old Bunyan House, I think. We used to go on the river. There was this part for children where they had little boats and two or three of us would get in. We had to turn the handles to work the boat and we had about half an hour. Then the man who owned the boat would shout out our number, 'Number six come back, come back,' so we had to get back. We used to love going to Bedford.

Lily Glazebrook

Heroine Tied to the Rails

We went to magic lantern shows at the Salvation Army. We used

Bunyan Baptist Sunday school outing to Bedford, 1929/30.

Hospital ball in the Town Hall, left to right, Mrs Glazebrook, Mrs Putnam, Mrs Roberts, ? Franklin, Mrs Abbiss, Mr Ashwood, mid-1930s.

to sit there and watch the trains come, when the heroine was tied to the rails – and the story of The Red Barn. We used to pay a few pence I think, not much. Who ran it, I don't know.

Patricia Smith

Mrs Grosvenor's Ball

Every year in the 1920s, Mrs Grosvenor, the old doctor's wife, used to hold a ball in the Town Hall. The girls used to use the the Council Chamber in which to get changed. This room was above stairs leading down by the side of the stage. I always danced one dance with Chetwynd Grosvenor. I was very small and young, not even in my teens and he was a tall young man.

Why I was allowed to go I don't know but, of course, my mother took me.

Eileen Harding

Rain on a Tin Roof

I loved the cinema, the Publix first of course. It had a tin roof and when it poured with rain then that would blot out the sound track. It was the first cinema I knew that had double, courting seats at the back. Much later, postwar, when the projectionist lived in Burymead he would start the projector on his way home from work. It was the old fashioned projector, it still used a carbon wick and as that burned down, of course, the screen got darker and darker so we all used to whistle which

117

alerted Mrs Kirby in the pay box, who would look through the door and then she would trot up to Burymead and the chap would get on his bike and come down.

Don Hills

Overspill Fair

They used to have a bit of Stevenage Fair in Franklin's Field, by the old Publix Cinema. Then they built on Franklin's Field and we had overspill of the Fair, in our field, for about ten or twelve years, I suppose. Our children loved it.

Roy Gates

Fair Days

I can remember in the early days of the fair, when they used to come with horses before they had so many big engines. They used to come round to the farm and say, 'Can I put two horses in your meadow?' and father would say, 'Yes,' and you'd go in the morning and there were twenty there! On fair days they used to come in and leave all the stuff over in Fairview Road and then they weren't allowed down until eight o'clock, when the hooter went at ESA. The best fighters had the best pitches. It wasn't marked out in those days, so those rough ones got the pick. We used to enjoy the fair more at that time. I'd be working at Aston End, near the pub and you could hear that music. Of course there wasn't the traffic and other noises. I used to love the music.

Stanley Marriott

Candyfloss and toffee-apple stall, Stevenage fair, 1960s.

Stevenage fair at the beginning of this century.

Bo-Peep

One Hospital Saturday, I remember Wendy Gates came round with a lovely lamb and on its back was a box for collecting and she was all dressed up as Bo-Peep. Her Mum was with her, with the lamb. It was lovely.

Patricia Smith

May I Have This Dance?

Dances were at the Town Hall of blessed memory, in Orchard Road, which was pulled down for the benefit of Lytton Way, and also at the ESA. They used to be more or less alternate Saturdays. We used to go to one one week, and one the other week. And also we went, fifty-fifty, dancing in the tin hut, or Parish Room, at the top of Basil's Road which were run by Ron Duberry's dad. George Briars used to do the Old Tyme and Ron Duberry's father used to run the modern. It was very good.

I had a dark suit with a stripe on it and I suppose I was a bit like a dummy really. It was all very formal, 'Please may I have this dance?' and all that sort of thing. It was all very nice. The big events were when you had live bands.

Wilf Neilson

The Piano Tuner

We also had a gramophone with a handle to wind it up. Mr Folbigg had a shop in the High Street where gramophone records could be purchased. Mr Watson's music shop was across the road from Folbigg's. He was a little, old-fashioned man with a bushy moustache, which was grey when I remember him. He used to go round on a bicycle, to tune pianos and I think

119

The Hospital Saturday procession outside the Yorkshire Grey, 1926.

Joan Hale as 'Silver Jubilee' and Jean Hale as a nurse, Hospital Saturday, 1935.

Advertisement for H.A. Watson, piano tuner, 1930s.

there was a time when he did ours. If we wanted to buy sheet music we went to Mr Watson's for it.

Joan Hale

Dancing Classes

Dancing in the Town Hall - oh, yes, that was a big thing. A man named Moore lived in the old Gas House, he taught us all dancing, and so did Mr Folbigg. I think the first dancing we ever did was in the tin hut in Stanmore Road. We had school meals in there too.

Roy Gates

A Pretty Dead Place

Leisure facilities in Stevenage really were non-existent. Whether or not it was an attractive town I don't know: attractive countryside around it – sure – but as a town a pretty dead place. I accepted that I was bored at times and the greatest thing that ever happened to Stevenage when I was a boy was the opening of the Astonia cinema in 1935 and the coming of Woolworth's in 1938. Stevenage was then a town – it had arrived.

Don Hills

'One Night of Love'

I can remember when the Astonia cinema first opened. My grandfather went. We thought he was old, but really I suppose he wasn't that old. He went to see Grace Moore in *One Night of Love* and my gran said, 'Silly old fool.'

Kathleen Jackson

Sausages in the Saxophone

We actually started a band. There was Den Boorman on the piano

121

accordion, John Boorman on the saxophone, in those days, and myself on drums and we had one or two other people, Billy Wittering on piano and John Clark, 'Nobby', on double bass and a chap joined us on saxophone and that was when John Boorman went on to guitar. Our first public gig was in January or February 1942 in St Ippolyts village hall – a memorable evening, with me all dolled up in my Uncle Arthur's old dress suit with a black bow, probably looking ridiculous when I think about it now, with a band that didn't take things very seriously. Nobby Clarke for instance played tricks with the saxophone player. The saxophone would suddenly make this weird honking noise and Nobby would go to the saxophone and look in the bell, put in his hand and pick out some sausages. It might had been funny, but it wasn't very good for the dancers as we discovered at our second gig which was at the village hall at Ickleford. We

had only been playing for about three quarters of an hour when the MC came to us and said, 'We are going to have an interval now. If you'd like to adjourn to the Cricketers and have yourselves a beer, I'll come and tell you when we are starting again.' Well we were in the Cricketers for about an hour and still no one came to tell us that the dance was starting, so I thought I'd better go and find out what was happening so I walked along to the village hall. As I got there I heard music and I thought that was odd because the band were in the pub and I went in and they had dragged a radiogram in and they were dancing to records. They preferred that to our band. Our fame went before us, because our next gig was at Pirton Village Hall and before we started the organiser asked me to go with him on a little walk and he took me to the village pond and said, 'Now, if we don't like the band that's where we put them.' So I impressed on the lads that they had to

Stevenage churches combined outing to Hunstanton, 1930/31.

be on their best behaviour that night –
no sausages out of the saxophone and
so on – so we got through that one all
right.

Don Hills

Day Out

We used to go to Mabelthorpe
or Skegness when we were at
Sunday school and they used to run a
train, the old steam train and that was
quite an occasion to go out for the day
then.

Kathleen Jackson

Football Outfits

We started up a football club in the
1930s, the Wednesday Football
Club. I was working in my father's shop,
that's why I had Wednesday afternoons
off – this was when the shops closed
on Wednesday afternoons. There was a
proper Wednesday League, the Luton
Wednesday League and Hitchin were
in it too. We played in the League and
we had cup ties, but I must say that we
didn't do very well in our first time. In
earlier days, previous to league football,
we arranged friendly matches to raise
money. I went to see Mr Day, the JP in
Walkern Road and he gave me a letter
sanctioning collections. When we could
afford it, we walked to Hitchin to the
football clothing place there, bought
our outfits and walked back again. I
was about sixteen when we started and
played for four seasons until the war
came. I played for the Stevenage Town

Reserves a couple of times. They hadn't
got a goalkeeper, so my father gave
me time off to play in goal for them. I
enjoyed that.

Norman Palmer

I Spent All My Time There

The Lytton Club was the big thing
really, to be quite honest, in my
life. It had opened in 1944 in Pound
Avenue. It was a brick building, built
by the Ministry of Works and partly
furnished on money provided by the
Women of America and it had a
cultural hall with a small stage. There
was a piano on it and a radiogram and
there was an office for the Warden
and the Assistant Warden and I spent
practically all my spare time there
organising different activities and
serving on the house committee as
secretary. At first it was only open to
Irish girls, then they were allowed to
bring in male guests and then in 1945 it
was opened up to anyone from the town
and eventually we became, I think,
Britain's first Citizens' Club.

Don Hills

ESA Fire

I was just going to Luton one day to
see the football and all of a sudden
we saw that fire at ESA and we went up
there and helped, climbed up handing
all this wood down, you know. I had my
best suit on too. That was a Saturday
afternoon and then later in the evening
the people came in top hats down from

Margaret Ashby (the author) in the arms of her mother, Edith, in their Pound Avenue garden, 1940. Next to it is the field where the Lytton Club was built a few years later and which is now occupied by Hammond Close and a number of flats.

The Lytton Club, Pound Avenue, c. 1960.

London, to have a look at it. And they sprayed the trains as they came through to stop the heat ruining the paintwork.

Stanley Marriott

Baby on Board

We used to go out on our bikes. Both of us had baby seats on our bikes, and then when the third child was a bit bigger, he used to ride along on his little tricycle. I remember going out and picking blackberries and then coming home and making blackberry and apple pies.

Kate Cope

Can You Sing?

My doctor, when we came to Stevenage, was Dr Deneys Swayne. If you went, as a newcomer, to Deneys Swayne, he didn't say, 'How are you?' He said, 'Can you sing and would you like to join the Lytton Players?' He worked damned hard in promoting the Lytton Players all round the town, all round the villages. I joined them in 1952 when we were in Alleyne's School, that's where we started and they also had a little hut in Pound Avenue. It had a very, very small stage and they used to put on quite small productions, mostly plays at that time, but we did put on one of the first Gilbert & Sullivan shows. I was in the chorus then and because there wasn't room in the hut, we had to change in a shed next to it. We used to play cards out there while the show was on and one of the entries was for total chorus to come on in *Pirates of Penzance*, I think it must have been. Of course, we all missed it and nobody came on at all. They were all playing poker.

Ray Gorbing

Cycling in the Rain

My brother started up a cycling club when I was sixteen. The first ride was out Bedford way and coming back it poured with rain. It was almost as far as I could go, quite a long ride for me. I went in for racing as well and I helped to start up another club and we met sometimes in the Marquess of Lorne. I became the Racing Secretary and there were several London cycling clubs' races that we entered. These were time trials of about twenty-five miles from Tempsford, up the North Road. We biked there first, which was about twenty-five miles to begin with, then raced twenty-five miles. But I quite enjoyed it and we had several wins. We had to leave early in the morning to get there, because they started at half-past six from Tempsford.

Norman Palmer

Dancing with Victor Sylvester

I had the great pleasure of dancing with Victor Sylvester once, when he came to the Mecca. It was when the Mecca first opened and he came down there several times. We were dancing, and we stopped and my husband said, 'My wife would like to dance with you,' and he did! When he came again, he always acknowledged us – he used to say, 'Hello, Mrs Gates.'

Mrs Gates

Loan Refused

It must have been in the late 1960s when we first had a car. I can remember my wife and I sitting and talking about how useful it would be to have a car. We could do a lot more with the children and we could also go home to South London by car. So I went to see the bank manager at Lloyds Bank and explained all this to him and he said, 'Oh no, I don't think you can afford a car at the moment, young man. You'll have to do without one.' It was a good year before I could persuade him to give me a loan.

John Amess

Long Stint

I met Dorothy Griffith, of the Red Cross in the clinic at 27, High Street. She was very involved in the Guide Movement and asked me, in the middle of a busy life, would I start looking after the 1st Stevenage Guide Company, because at that time there was no leader. So I said, 'Well, I can't possibly take it on as a permanent job. I'll just do it for a few weeks.' 'Yes,' she said, 'Just two or three weeks and we shall find another Guider.' But the two or three weeks developed into twenty-six years. Somehow I wangled my holidays so that I could go to camp. I also got involved with the Rangers and went to Denmark with

them. That only happened because they couldn't go to Denmark unless they had someone qualified in first aid. We went to camp once a year. The one thing I jibbed at was night hikes with the Scouts and I wouldn't take the responsibility for that.

Stella Kestin

Sold Out

Music Hall was one of the most popular things we did in the olden days and in fact when we were in the college we played for a whole week. There were 310 seats there and they were sold out. There was a waiting list for people.

Ray Gorbing

Theatrical designer

Mostly I was interested in amateur drama and I began to design stage sets for the Bancroft Players. I did some stage sets for, what was then in Stevenage, the Lytton Players. I'd always had an interest in theatrical design and had ambitions in that direction, I suppose. I spent most of my weekends and evenings painting stage sets and designing them and making models.

Peter Blagg

No Baby-Sitter

I did belong to the Lytton Players, but not for very long because I had a husband who was always working long hours and I had no one to baby-sit. Although people baby sat for each other, I somehow didn't get involved in that. We were a bit old-fashioned, my husband and I, and believed in looking after our own children, so I had to drop out of the Lytton Players.

Kate Cope

Composer Was There

Pam, my wife, sang with the Orchard Singers and I often tell people about that, because I can remember going and collecting her from Barnwell School one evening and who should be there but the composer, John Rutter. The Orchard Singers were the first people to actually sing John Rutter's Shepherds' Pipe Carol and that was when those carols were still in manuscript. John Rutter was Director of Music at Clare College, Cambridge and from there he became a free-lance composer. Simon Marlow was the conductor of the Orchard Singers and it was he who brought John Rutter along for this Christmas concert.

Alan Cudmore

The Faithful Horse

In 1959, I went with my father, Arthur Hale, for a very enjoyable pony trekking holiday. I had never ridden before, but Dad, who was then 66, had been a groom at Walkern Hall in his younger days. After the holiday, we went to see Mr Fred Allen at Chesfield Manor Farm, who ran a riding school and arranged to go hacking once a week. We were taken through the surrounding beautiful countryside and lanes, now sadly, much built over. We enjoyed it so much that we continued until Dad had to go into hospital in 1973, only a few weeks short of eighty years of age. Of course, there were many children at the riding school and dad greatly enjoyed their company. He particularly loved to ride a large mare called Grace who, I believe, had once been a cart horse. When she was old and in failing health, Mr Allen delayed the time when she was 'put to sleep' by a few days, in order that Dad could ride her for the last time.

Joan Hale

Arthur Hale at Chesfield riding stables.

More Spare Time

In 1972, when the children were beginning to get off hand and I was beginning to have a little more spare time in the evening, I was looking round for something to do. I had always been interested in local history and so I went along to the Stevenage Society meetings. In those days they met in Stevenage College and when I arrived I found that there were, in fact, only six members at that time and they promptly elected me secretary.

John Amess

Strictly for the Birds

I was quite a keen bird-watcher at that stage and was a founder member of the Stevenage and District Ornithological Society with Ian Purdy, who was a planner at the Development Corporation. We used to have, during the winter, meetings in the hall of the Methodist Church in Sish Lane. The Ornithological Society flourished for quite a few years and we used to have weekend outings to places like Dungeness Power Station, to see Black Redstarts.

Alan Cudmore

Favourite Walks

On our family walks we used to go up Sish Lane to Shephall and back through Whomerley Wood. Another walk was to Norton Green, going down London Road over the Langley siding bridge and meeting probably the Nash family coming back from their walk. One walk which we particularly enjoyed and why we were also against the expansion of Stevenage was to Norton Green, through the wood there, where the wood-yard is and down to Dyes Farm, over to the public house along there, the Royal Oak. Then we'd go across fields there past Titmuss's farm to get home. Or across into Norton Green coming down through Symonds Green then over Fishers Green and the lovely woods behind there and back across Halfpenny Bridge. Everybody used to walk.

Norman Palmer